STUDIES IN THE PSALMS

STUDIES IN THE PSALMS

By the late

S. R. DRIVER, D.D.

Regius Professor of Hebrew, and Canon of Christ Church, Oxford;
Hon. D.Litt. Cambridge and Dublin; Hon. D.D. Glasgow
and Aberdeen; Fellow of the British Academy;
Corresponding Member of the Royal Prussian
Academy of Sciences.

Edited, with a Preface, by

C. F. BURNEY, D.Litt.

Oriel Professor of the Interpretation of Holy Scripture in the
University of Oxford.

Wipf and Stock Publishers
199 West 8th Avenue, Suite 3
Eugene, Oregon 97401

Studies in the Psalms
By Driver, S.R.
ISBN: 1-59244-461-X
Publication date 1/12/2004
Previously published by Hodder and Stoughton, 1915

PREFACE

THE present volume is published in accordance with the wish expressed by Dr. Driver, shortly before his death, that I should bring together and edit his scattered studies on the Psalms. He expressly mentioned the articles entitled 'The Method of Studying the Psalter,' which appeared in the *Expositor*, January-July, 1910, the article on the Prayer Book Version of the Psalter which he contributed to the Prayer Book Dictionary, and the sermon (hitherto unpublished) on the 'Imprecatory' Psalm cix. To these I have added other sermons on the Psalms, selected from unpublished sermons which were placed at my disposal by Mrs. Driver. These are all the sermons on the Psalms which he left, except such as had already been utilized by him for the *Expositor* articles. They were all preached at

PREFACE

Christ Church Cathedral at various periods during his residence as Canon ; and since they afford practical illustration of the method of interpretation which he lays down in the published articles, their inclusion in the volume appeared particularly suitable.

The bringing together of this varied material bearing on the one subject has almost necessarily involved a small amount of repetition ; e.g. the teaching of the sermon on Psalm cix is summarized in Section 13 of the article on the Prayer Book Version of the Psalter ; while the sermon on Psalm lxxii to some extent repeats the interpretation of the same Psalm in the *Expositor* articles, but has been included on account of the valuable application which it contains (pp. 270 ff.) to the occasion for which it was written—the Coronation of our present King.

The volume should form a welcome example of one side of Dr. Driver's activity which was prominent throughout his career— the application of the results of minute and scientific study of the Old Testament to the popular need. The research into the language

PREFACE

and contents of the Old Testament which formed his life-work was for him no merely linguistic and literary exercise. He was always keenly conscious of the living voice of God speaking throughout the pages of the Scriptures ; and he sought, by all the means at his disposal, not merely to lay down a sound basis of interpretation for trained scholars, but also to utilize the outcome of his scholarship for the furtherance of practical Religion—to emphasize and make clear the spiritual gain which results from a sober and reverent use of the means and methods of Old Testament study which the researches of scholars like himself have placed within the reach of all.

The canons of his method of interpretation may be said to be twofold ; the minute and scholarly exposition of the text of the Psalm with which he is dealing, and the endeavour accurately to ascertain the character of the historical situation by which it was called forth and the meaning which it was intended to convey to those for whom it was written. So interpreted, the permanent spiritual application of the Psalms will be found, for the

PREFACE

most part, to spring directly out of the writer's exposition ; and it was not his method to labour and expand his conclusion, which is commonly as terse and summary as it is directly to the point.

It has seemed worth while to compile an Index as a ready means of reference for students of the Psalms. My thanks are due to Sir Isaac Pitman and Sons, the publishers of the Prayer Book Dictionary, for permission to republish the article on the Prayer Book Version of the Psalter, and to the Editor of the *Expositor* for similar permission in regard to the articles first published in his periodical.

C. F. BURNEY.

Oxford, 1915.

CONTENTS

PART I   PAGE

The Prayer Book Version of the Psalter .   3

PART II

The Method of Studying the Psalter, with
    Special Application to some of the Messianic Psalms 33

    Introduction 33

    Psalm ii 51

CONTENTS

	PAGE
Psalm xlv	77
Psalm lxxii	97
Psalm cx	115
Psalm xl	135
Psalm xxii	155
Psalm xvi	189

PART III

Sermons on the Psalms

Psalm cix	213
Psalm viii	231

CONTENTS

	PAGE
Psalm xv	247
Psalm lxxii	265
Psalm lxxiii	281
INDEX	303

THE PRAYER BOOK VERSION OF
THE PSALTER

THE PRAYER BOOK VERSION OF THE PSALTER

THE Prayer Book Version of the Psalms is, in all essentials, the version contained in the so-called *Great Bible* of 1539–41. Tindale (*c.* 1485–1536) had produced in 1530 the first English version of the Pentateuch translated from the original Hebrew; Miles Coverdale (1488–1569) had published in 1535 his English version of the entire Bible; and a composite version, by Thomas Matthew, a combination of Tindale's and Coverdale's had appeared in 1537. Thomas Cromwell, Earl of Essex, at that time chief minister of Henry VIII, had set his heart on the production of an amended version of the Bible in English; he accordingly invited Coverdale to prepare a revised translation, based on a more accurate collation of the Hebrew and Greek originals. Coverdale was assisted

1. Sources of P.B. Version.

THE PRAYER BOOK VERSION

in his task by 'dyverse excellent learned men'; and the result of their joint labours appeared in April, 1539. An Injunction, published by Cromwell with the King's authority, required a copy to be set up in some convenient place in every church in the kingdom before a specified day. The interest taken in the new Bible was remarkable; crowds flocked to every church to read, or hear read, the hitherto unknown book. The *Great Bible* as it was already called in view of its 'greater volume,' by its publisher, Grafton, well deserved the name; it is a magnificent blackletter folio, of some 1,050 pages. A second edition, revised especially in the prophetical and poetical books, followed in April, 1540, and five others in July and November, 1540, and May, November, and December, 1541.

The text which was taken as the basis of the *Great Bible* was that of Matthew's Bible

2. The Great Bible.
(1537); and this was revised by Coverdale with the help of Sebastian Münster's Latin version of the Old Testament (Heidelberg, 1534–5)—an important version in which much use was

made of the mediaeval Jewish commentators, and which exerted considerable influence upon subsequent English translators. Coverdale also naturally introduced improvements of his own. In the case of the Psalms the text of Matthew's composite Bible thus revised was Coverdale's own former translation of 1535.

A single example (Ps. xix. 7) must suffice to illustrate the nature of Coverdale's revision; the influence of Sebastian Münster, it will be seen, is very marked. Coverdale, 1535, and Matthew, 1537 : 'The Law of the Lord is a *perfect* law; it *quickeneth* the soul : the testimony of the Lord is *true*, and giveth wisdom, *even* unto *babes*.' Sebastian Münster, 1534-5 : 'Lex domini *immaculata*, *convertens* animam : testimonium domini *firmum*, sapienter erudiens *simplicem*.' Great Bible, 1539-41 : 'The law of the Lord is an *undefiled* law, *converting* the soul; the testimony of the Lord is *sure*, and giveth wisdom unto the *simple*.' (For another good example, see Kirkpatrick's note on Psalm cv. 18.)

The seven editions of the *Great Bible*, while

THE PRAYER BOOK VERSION

exhibiting substantially the same text, differ frequently in details, as alterations, based largely upon Münster, were from time to time introduced, especially in April, 1540. Thus in Psalm xxxii. 7, where the edition of 1539 had 'in due season,' that of April, 1540, had 'in a time when thou mayest be found,' based upon Münster's 'in tempore quo invenire (te licet).' Psalm cxliii. 3 'as the men that have been long dead'—(first in 1540)—comes from the same source.

At the time when both the First (1549) and Second (1552) Prayer Books of Edward VI were set forth, the *Great Bible* was still the authorised English translation of the Scriptures ; it was but natural therefore that the version of the Psalms contained in it should be expressly appointed as the one to be used in the daily services of the Church. And when, at the last revision of the Prayer Book in 1662, it was directed that the other lessons from Scripture should be taken from the Authorised Version of 1611, an exception was made in the case of the Psalter : choirs and congregations were alike familiar with it,

OF THE PSALTER

and it was felt to be 'smoother and more easy to sing.'

The Psalter, however, as printed in modern Prayer Books, is not an exact reprint of the Psalter of any of the seven editions of the *Great Bible*. Substantially it agrees with the later editions; but small variations have been from time to time introduced into editions of the Prayer Book Psalter, mostly by the early printers, apparently without any authority, but often, it seems, suggested by a comparison with some other version (such as the text of the *Great Bible* Psalter incorporated in the *Bishops' Bible* of 1568, and the Authorised Version of 1611). Modern Psalters, it has been shown, follow very closely texts contained in a *Great Bible* (4to) of 1569, a *Bishops' Bible* of 1591 and a Prayer Book Psalter of 1583: see especially the Appendix to McGarvey's *Liturgiae Americanae*, Philadelphia, 1895, pp. 1*–51*, by the Rev. F. Gibson, D.D., containing a detailed tabulated synopsis of various readings in more than 500 passages, collected from some 60 editions of the *Great*

3. Relation of P.B. Version to Great Bible Psalter.

THE PRAYER BOOK VERSION

Bible and Prayer Book Psalter dating from 1539 to 1892. At the present time (1911), the *authorised* text of the Prayer Book Psalter is that which was adopted in the revised Prayer Book accepted by Convocation in 1661 and, from its having been annexed in MS. to the Act of Uniformity in 1662, known as the *Annexed Prayer Book*. A *facsimile* of the *Annexed* Book was published by Eyre & Spottiswoode in 1891. Certain printed copies of this *Annexed Prayer Book*, certified as correct (though, as a matter of fact, they do not always agree with the *Annexed Prayer Book* : see below ; and cp. the writer's *Parallel Psalter*, ed. 2, 1904, p. xliv., n.) under the Great Seal in 1662, are called, in consequence, the *Sealed Books* (see, for these, Stephens' elaborate annotated edition of 1854). Many of the changes spoken of above as gradually introduced into the Prayer Book Psalter were adopted in the *Annexed Prayer Book*, and thus implicitly sanctioned ; there are some also which were made in the *Annexed Book* for the first time. A few examples may be cited (G.B. 1–2, etc. = first, second, etc., edition

OF THE PSALTER

of the *Great Bible* : **A.B.**=the *Annexed Book*). The statements following are made on the authority of Dr. Gibson's synopsis.

Psalm xiii. 2 : ' Mine enemy,' G.B. 1-7 (so Heb.) ; ' mine enemies,' first in a P. of 1548. Psalm xxxviii. 10 : ' The light of mine eyes,' G.B. 1-7 (so Heb.) ; ' the sight of mine eyes,' first in a P. of 1574 (a mere misprint, due to the resemblance of the black letters s to l, but continued to the present day). Psalm xl. 6 : ' Thy wondrous works ' G.B. 1-7 (so Heb.) ; ' the wondrous works,' first in A.B. Psalm xlviii. 10 : ' Daughters of Judah,' G.B. 1-7 (so Heb.) ; ' daughter of Judah,' first in A.B. Psalm lxxxvii. 4 : ' Behold,[1] yee (i.e. yea) the Philistines also,' G.B. 1, 2, 3 ; ' behold ye the Philistines also,' first in G.B. 4, and generally in subsequent editions. Psalm xcv. 7 : ' Sheep of his hands,' G.B. 1-7, and subsequently, including A.B. ; ' sheep of his hand,' first in the *Sealed Books*. Psalm cxlv. 3 : ' Marvellous worthy ' (' marvellous ' being an adverb, as in Psalm xxxi. 23), G.B. 1-7, etc., and A.B. ; ' mar-

[1] Here an interjection, as in the Hebrew, not a verb.

THE PRAYER BOOK VERSION

vellous, worthy,' an error first in the *Sealed Books*, and found still in most modern Prayer Books. One misprint *yea* for *Jah*, in Psalm lxviii. 4, already found in G.B. 2, remained in editions and Prayer Books (including the *Annexed Book* and *Sealed Books*) till it was corrected in 1701. Some of the changes consisted in the removal of archaisms : thus Psalm xxxii. 5, ' I will *knowledge* my sin unto thee,' and Psalm civ. 21, ' To seek their meat *at* God,' were both first altered in the *Annexed Book*. ' Mowes,' an old word meaning *grimaces* in Psalm xxxv. 15, was also first changed into ' mouths ' in the *Annexed Book*.

In the *Great Bible* certain words and passages not in the Hebrew (e.g. Psalm xiii. 6 ; ' bring young rams unto the Lord ' in xxix. 1 ; and ' God ' in xlv. 12), but additions or glosses, derived often from the Vulgate, are printed in smaller type ; and in the *Annexed Book* these passages, and also some others not in the Hebrew, are all enclosed within square brackets. These distinguishing marks have, however, been gradually dropped in modern

OF THE PSALTER

Prayer Books; and they have now, unfortunately, entirely disappeared.[1]

Coverdale must have been a natural master of English Style. His version of the Psalms, in the form in which it appears in the *Great Bible*, is wonderfully attractive: its style is bold and vigorous, and at the same time flowing and melodious; and its diction, while thoroughly idiomatic and of genuinely native growth, is dignified and chaste. It is not surprising that it has endeared itself to many generations of Churchmen. But it is unfortunately disfigured by serious inaccuracies: it also contains renderings which blunt and obscure the meaning of a Psalm or passage; and there are many words in it (e.g. 'grudge,' 'froward,' 'conversation,' 'health,' 'worship') which are now either obsolete, or have changed their meaning, and are thus not understood. Those who love, and habitually use, the Prayer Book Psalter have a claim to be able to learn from it the sense of

4. Style and character of P.B. Version.

[1] They have been restored in the writer's *Parallel Psalter*.

THE PRAYER BOOK VERSION

the original more exactly than they can at present do ; and a gentle and conservative revision, which, while jealously guarding its unrivalled beauties of rhythm and diction, would enable them to do this, is a much needed desideratum.[1]

In so far as the Psalter forms a part of the Prayer Book, its use is *devotional* ; and the question of the dates and authors of individual Psalms becomes a matter of secondary importance. Still, it deserves a few words here. The Psalms are seldom as impersonal as a modern hymn. They often describe the writer's experience ; they allude to, or even celebrate, historical events. They thus invite us, if we can, to realize the situation

5. Dates and Authors of Psalms.

---

[1] See further, on the sources of the Prayer Book Version, Driver, *Parallel Psalter*, Introduction ; Westcott, *History of the English Bible* (ed. 2, 1872 ; ed. 3, 1905), c. ii. §§ 2–4, and c. iii. §§ 2–4 ; Lupton in Hastings' *Dictionary of the Bible*, v. 244–8. Cp. W. A. Wright, *The Hexaplar Psalter* (1911), containing the versions of Coverdale (1535), the Great Bible (1539), the Geneva Bible (1560), the Bishops' Bible (1568), the Authorised Version and the Revised Version, printed in parallel columns.

OF THE PSALTER

out of which they sprang. Moreover, as the religion of the Old Testament developed historically, the intelligent worshipper should have some idea of the period of history to which the several Psalms belong. Their actual dates we can, indeed, only determine broadly ; of their authors, beyond the fact that a small nucleus is probably Davidic, we know nothing. The Psalter, it is evident, assumed its present form gradually. In the Hebrew text (as in the Revised Version) it is divided into five *Books* (viz., Psalms i.–xli., xlii.–lxxii., lxxiii.–lxxxix., xc.–cvi., cvii.–cl.), which in their turn include smaller collections, as the seventy-three 'Davidic' Psalms (not all grouped together), the twelve Psalms of Asaph, etc. Very few Psalms are earlier than the seventh century B.C. ; and the great majority are exilic or post-exilic. Of the seventy-three Psalms ascribed to David, internal evidence —the situation presupposed, or the ideas, or sometimes the lateness of the Hebrew—shows that certainly the greater number are of much later date.[1] The Psalter reflects the

[1] See, for the grounds of these statements, the writer's

THE PRAYER BOOK VERSION

religious feelings and experiences of a long succession of pious men in Israel ; and it is no doubt to this diversity of origin that it owes its extraordinary variety of mood, and style, and theme.

But, though we can seldom or never fix the actual author or occasion of a Psalm we can often reconstruct—at least in Psalms of a personal character—from the allusions and terms used, the *kind* of situation in which the author was, and out of which the Psalm sprang. It is essential to make an effort to do this, if we wish to understand the aim and object of the Psalm in question. There is great variety in the situations presupposed by the Psalms. In Psalm iii. the Psalmist is surrounded by foes, who unite in declaring that there is no help for him in his God ; but he appeals with confidence to Jehovah, who has defended him hitherto, and foretells the discomfiture of his assailants. In Psalm iv. the author is

6. Personal situation implied in many Psalms.

Introduction to the Literature of the Old Testament, pp. 373–387.

surrounded by impatient and distrustful companions, who blame him for some misfortune which has befallen them : he bids them regain a right frame of mind, and trust : in the joy of faith he himself can lie down and rest securely. In Psalm xi. society is in disorder : in the confusion the lives of the righteous are imperilled : the poet's despondent friends urge him to seek safety in flight : it is hopeless to attempt to stem the tide of anarchy. The Psalmist replies in tones of calm and unabated confidence in Jehovah. In Psalm xlii.-xliii., the author is somewhere in the Hermon region ('concerning' in the Prayer Book Version of $v.$ 8 is a misrendering of Sebastian Münster's *de*, 'from'), and debarred from worshipping in the Temple ; he is taunted by heathen foes with being deserted by his God. With great pathos, he utters his yearnings for God, recalls the happiness of the past, and prays earnestly for restoration to the privileges of the sanctuary. And similarly in many other cases. The situation thus reconstructed often throws much light on the gist and meaning of a Psalm.

THE PRAYER BOOK VERSION

In the Psalter the ripest fruits of Israel's spiritual experience are gathered together, and the religious affections find their richest and fullest expressions. The Psalms are pre-eminently *devotional* in character : and the soul is displayed in them in converse with God, disclosing to Him its manifold emotions, its hopes and fears, its desires and aspirations ; we hear in it, for instance, the voices of distress and despair, of confession and supplication, of confidence and faith, of yearning for the sanctuary (Psalms xlii.–xliii., lxiii., lxxxiv.), of love and devotion, of thanksgiving, triumph, and adoration ; we hear in it meditations on the Divine attributes—as shown in nature or history, in the problems of human life (Psalms xxxvii., xlix., lxxiii.), in the pathos of human existence (Psalms xxxix., xc.) ; and we hear all these notes uttered with a depth and intensity and a beauty of diction and rhythm, which secure for the Psalter a unique place in religious literature. In the Psalms, moreover, it is to be noted that love, and reverence, and trust, and other sacred affections are

7. Religious value of Psalter.

OF THE PSALTER

not, as in most parts of the Old Testament, enjoined as a duty from without, but are set before us as a spontaneous outcome of a heart filled with the spirit of God and stirred by devout emotions. It is the surprising variety of mood and subject and occasion in the Psalms, combined with their deep spirituality, their fullness of human feeling, their ready applicability (though see § 13) to the needs and situations of practically all men in all ages, and a literary form such as all can appreciate, which gives them their catholicity, and adapts them to form the hymn book not only of the second Temple but of the Christian Church.

In *interpreting* a Psalm, there are two or three important considerations which must be borne in mind. In the first place, we have sometimes to ask ourselves who the speaker is: is it an individual, or the nation? Secondly, it must be remembered that every Psalm springs out of the Psalmist's own time, and bears, more or less distinctly, the marks of that time ; and many Psalms, as we have already partly seen, allude distinctly to the

8. Canons of Interpretation.

THE PRAYER BOOK VERSION

circumstances of the author, or of the persons addressed, or spoken of, in them. As will appear in §§ 10–12, these personal references in a Psalm have often an important bearing on its interpretation. Thirdly, in interpreting the Psalms, if we are to keep on sure ground, a distinction must be clearly drawn between the original sense of a passage and an application which may be made of it : a Psalm or part of Psalm may be *applied* to many persons and many situations, which were entirely out of the mind of its author ; and we must be careful not to apply a Psalm in such a way as to confuse the *application* with the *interpretation*. Moreover, a Psalm is a *unity* ; and though it may, in parts, be *applied* to many different persons, it must, as a *whole*, have been referred by its author to the same person (or persons).

The *speaker* in the Psalms is mostly, no doubt, the individual Psalmist, but sometimes it is the *nation*, in whose name the Psalmist speaks. This is the case not only where the pronouns are in the first person *plural*, but also

9. The Speaker in the Psalms.

sometimes where they are in the first person *singular*: for Hebrew idiom often uses a singular verb or pronoun of a people: see e.g. Exodus xiv. 25 (in the Hebrew, 'And Egypt said, Let *me* flee'), Numbers xx. 18, 19; Isaiah. xii. 1, 2; xxv. 1; Psalm cxxix. 1-3; Lamentations iii. The nation is thus the speaker in Psalms xliv. 5, 7, 16; lx. 9; lxvi. 12-18 (cp. *us, our, vv.* 8-11); lxxiv. 13; lxxxix. 49; xciv. 16-19, 22; cii.; cxviii.; and perhaps in some other Psalms, as Psalms ix.-x., lvi. (notice how the speaker's foes here are not individuals, but *nations, v.* 7 R.V.), lvii. There are also probably many cases in which a Psalm has a *representative* character, and in which the Psalmist speaks not only in his own name, but also in that of his godly, and often persecuted, co-religionists, whose experiences and emotions he feels as his own. And in Psalm xxii. it is probable that the speaker, from whose deliverance such far-reaching consequences for the world are deduced (*v.* 27 ff.), is faithful or 'ideal' Israel, the ideal 'servant of Jehovah' of Isaiah xlii. 1-4;

xlix. 1–9; l. 4–9; lii. 13—liii. 12 (cp. especially Isaiah xlix. 6, 7).

The *Messianic* Psalms in the proper sense of the expression (for the term *Messiah* means specifically the 'anointed' king), are those which depict an Israelite king under a more or less *ideal* character; and it is in virtue of this ideal character which they attribute to him that they are *Messianic*. The Psalms in which this ideal element is most prominent are Psalms ii., xlv., lxxii., cx.; other Psalms in which it is slighter are Psalms xviii. (see *vv.* 43–5), xxi. (*v.* 4), lxi. (*vv.* 6, 7); and cp. also lxxxix. 20–36 and cxxxii. 11–19. These Psalms, though they refer primarily to the circumstances of the time, and speak throughout of the actual king,[1] represent him as invested with various ideal attributes and powers—e.g. victorious over distant foes,

10. Messianic Psalms

[1] Psalms ii., lxxii., cx., *may*, however, be entirely pictures of the future ideal king, constructed on the basis of earlier prophetic delineations; but even these are strongly coloured by contemporary references; and the pictures drawn in them, however idealized, are only the rule or conquests of an *earthly* Israelite king.

ruling to the ends of the earth, securing for his subjects justice and peace—such as were never possessed by any actual Israelite king, and which thus point onward to a future *ideal* king. In what sense, however, are these Psalms fulfilled by Christ ? A careful study of prophecy shows that Christ 'does not so much fulfil predictions as realize ideals' (cp. Edghill, *Evidential Value of Prophecy*, 1906, pp. 435 f., 483 f.) ; and the Messianic Psalms contain, not predictions, but *ideals*. They are not predictions of a future Christ, partly because they refer evidently (with the possible exceptions mentioned in note ¹) to one or other contemporary king, and partly because they all (without exception) describe an *earthly* rule, and so contain many features which Christ did not fulfil. The Hero of the Psalms, for instance, fights against earthly armies, his slain cover the plain (Ps. cx. 6), his rule is one of iron (Ps. ii. 9), he marries and has children, who represent him in different parts of the dominion (Ps. xlv. 17). Christ 'fulfils' these ideals not in a literal, but in a spiritual, sense. He discards the temporary, 'dispensational' elements—i.e. the elements belonging to the Jewish dispensation—and realizes the essential idea of kingly character, of which the ideal is the expression. (See further, on the whole question of the manner in which our Lord 'fulfils' prophecy, with especial reference to quotations in the New Testament, Edghill, op. cit., pp. 399-573 ; and, on the idea of the term 'fulfil,' pp. 435 f., 483 f.)

There are other Psalms also which express ideals realized by Christ ; but, as they do not depict an ideal *king*, they can be termed *Messianic* only in a broader and less exact sense. Thus Psalm viii. represents man as holding an ideal dominion over the world ; Psalms xv. and xxiv. 1-6 delineate (in outline) an ideal godly character ; Psalm xvi. expresses an ideal, both of fellowship with God, and of superiority to death ; in Psalm xxii. the speaker, probably (see § 9) faithful Israel, while plainly in *vv.* 1-21 describing his own personal sufferings, attributes to his deliverance a world-wide signifi-

[marginal note: 11. Psalms containing other Ideal Features.]

OF THE PSALTER

cance (*v.* 27 ff.). Of these Psalms, though none in their original import relate to Christ, Psalm xxii. is *Messianic* (in the sense just explained) in being 'fulfilled' by Him, as the genuine impersonation of ideal Israel; the others are so, only in the sense that they describe ideals which He realizes more completely than ordinary men. The godly Israelite, and the representative men of Israel—especially in the Psalms, the king, and, though less conspicuously, the prophet—were, under different aspects, types of Christ—of course partial and imperfect types, but still types; and the Psalms in which their experiences, their aspirations and their ideals are expressed are thus (to speak technically) 'typically' *Messianic* (see especially Perowne, *The Psalms*, Introduction, chap. iii. ed. 1886, pp. 49-55). Naturally, we must recognize a Divine control, determining the line of the Psalmists' thoughts, and enabling them thus in all such Psalms to foreshadow the future Christ.

Other Psalms give expression to the great prophetic ideal (Isaiah ii. 2-4, etc.), of a future conversion of the Gentiles to the true God

THE PRAYER BOOK VERSION

(xxii. 27, 28, xlvii. 9, lxv. 2, lxvi. 3, lxvii., lxviii. 29, 31, lxxxvi. 9, lxxxvii., cii. 15, 21 f. : cp. the invitations to the nations to praise God, xlvii. 1, 6–8, lxvi. 1, 7–10, c., etc.); and they thus foreshadow the intended results of the diffusion of the Gospel in the world.

The primary import of the Psalms is often misunderstood through the use made of them in the New Testament. But it is necessary to bear in mind the principles on which the Old Testament is often quoted in the New Testament. Passages are often *applied* to Christ though they do not primarily refer either to Him, or even to the Jewish Messiah, because they describe a situation similar to one in which He was placed, or because they are true of Him in a fuller and more comprehensive sense than they are of those of whom they were originally spoken. Thus Psalm xli. 9 is said in John xiii. 18 to be 'fulfilled' by Christ. The verse, where it stands, in Psalm xli., refers actually to the false friend of the author of the Psalm and to no one else. Christ cannot, as is some-

12. Application Distinct from Interpretation.

OF THE PSALTER

times strangely supposed, be the speaker in the Psalm [1] because of the confession of sin in *v.* 4 and because of the unchristian prayer in *v.* 10: 'Raise me up (from my bed of sickness) *that I may requite them.*' All that is meant in the quotation is that the experience of the godly sufferer of old is repeated, in the case of Christ, in a keener form. Psalm xxxv. 19 is quoted similarly in John xv. 25; but the Psalm cannot as a whole be referred to Christ, because it contains much (including imprecations, *vv.* 8, 26) which would be quite unsuitable in His mouth. Psalm xl. 8-10, again, is in Hebrews x. 5-7 quoted as referring to Christ. But it must be obvious that the Psalm, in its original intention, has no reference to Christ: it is some Old Testament saint, not Christ, who declares that it is his delight to do God's will; and in *v.* 15 the Psalmist speaks of his 'sins,' which, except by most strained and unnatural exegesis, can be understood only as the iniquities which he has himself committed. But the ideal of obedience, expressed in *vv.* 8-10, is *applied*

[1] Cp., on this subject, Perowne, l.c., pp. 41–50.

THE PRAYER BOOK VERSION

to Christ, as a fitting expression of His perfect conformity to His Father's will. The same may be said of Psalms liv. and lxix. These Psalms, though they may in parts be *applied* to Christ, and are thus suitably read on Good Friday, cannot, as wholes, be referred to Him : notice liv. 5, the prayer for the destruction of the Psalmist's enemies ; liv. 7, the thought of gratified vengeance ; lxix. 5, the confession of sin ; lxix. 23–29, the imprecations. Psalms viii., xv., xvi., xxiv. 1–6, have been sufficiently considered above.[1]

13. Imprecatory Psalms.

Only the so-called *Imprecatory Psalms* seem to form an exception to what has been said above on the high spiritual value of the Psalter, and its ready adaptability to give direction and expression to the devotional feelings of Christian men. The imprecations in the Psalms (principally xxxv. 4–8, lix. 11–13,

[1] See further on §§ 10–12, Perowne and Kirkpatrick on the Psalms quoted ; W. T. Davison, *The Praises of Israel* (an Introduction to the Study of the Psalms), pp. 201–254 ; Perowne, Introduction, l.c., pp. 62–5 ; Kirkpatrick, Introduction, p. lviii. ff. ; and the succeeding studies in the present volume.

lxix. 23-29, cix. 5-19—cp. also lviii. 9, cxxxvii. 9) strike a discordant note in a book which breathes in general a spirit of saintly resignation. In the case of Psalm cix., it has been supposed that *vv.* 5-19 are not the curses of the Psalmist himself, but those of his *enemies*, which he quotes (so that ' saying ' should be understood at the end of *v.* 4). It is doubtful if this view is correct (notice *v.* 19) ; but, even if it were, the principle would not account for the other imprecations in the Psalms, or for the hardly less strong ones expressed by Jeremiah (xi. 20, xvii. 18, xviii. 21-23 ; cp. also the glow of *national* vengeance which animates Isaiah xxxiv., Jeremiah l. 2-li. 58). Such utterances may be palliated ; but it is idle to pretend that they breathe the spirit of Christ, or that they can be appropriated consistently by His followers. They may be palliated in part by the consideration that the Psalmists, like the prophets, were keenly sensible of the great conflict going on between Good and Evil, between God and His enemies, both as between Israel and heathen nations, and as between the godly and the ungodly in Israel itself; they felt that the cause really at stake was the very existence of all divine truth and righteousness upon earth : in desiring, therefore, the downfall of their ungodly enemies, they were but desiring the overthrow of evil in the world, and the triumph of righteousness and the cause of truth. Even, however, when full allowance has been made for such considerations, there remains a *personal* element, an element of personal feeling and vindictiveness, which cannot be eliminated. The foes of the Psalmist or of Jeremiah may have been hostile to a cause ; but they also attacked and persecuted a *person* ; and it is the personal feeling thus aroused which finds expression in these imprecations, and which also, judged by the standard of Christian ethics, stands condemned. We must admit it ; and can only see it in the voice of persecuted righteousness, not yet freed from discordant notes by the precept and example of Christ. The Old Testament contains the record of a *progressive* revelation : the education of the chosen nation was gradual : there is a human element in the Biblical writers, which inspiration elevates and illumines, but does not suppress ; it ought not therefore to surprise us if human feeling, which is so prominent in Old Testament writers, and as a rule is so singularly pure and noble, should occasionally betray its earthly origin. (See further, Perowne on the Psalms quoted ; Kirkpatrick, p. lxxxviii. ff. ; Bruce, *Apologetics*, p. 329 f.) ; and the sermon included in the present volume, pp. 213 ff.

Literature (selected)—Perowne, *The Psalms*, ed. 6, 1886 ; Kirkpatrick in the *Cambridge Bible*

13. Literature.
(1892) ; Baethgen (the best recent German commentary), ed. 2, 1904 ; W. T. Davison, *The Praises of Israel*, 1893, the article *Psalms* in Hastings' *Dictionary of the Bible* ; Sanday, Bampton Lectures on *Inspiration*, 1893, Lecture IV ; Westcott, *The Paragraph Psalter*, 1881 ; Driver, *The Parallel Psalter*, ed. 2, 1904 (the Prayer Book Version and a new version arranged on opposite pages, with Introduction and Glossaries explaining words and phrases occurring frequently in the Psalms and archaisms

THE PRAYER BOOK VERSION

in the Prayer Book Version) ; Carleton, *The Psalter of the Church*, 1909 (the Prayer Book Version with Introduction and notes explaining or correcting the Prayer Book Version where necessary) ; Oesterley, *The Psalms in the Jewish Church*, 1910 (including use in the Temple and Synagogue) ; Cheyne, *The Devout Study of Criticism*, 1892, p. 129 ff. (sermon-studies on selected Psalms) ; R. W. Church, in the *Gifts of Civilization*, 1880, p. 391 ff. ; Ottley, Bampton Lectures on *Aspects of the Old Testament*, 1897, p. 350 ff. ; W. E. Barnes, *Lex in Corde* (Studies in the Psalter), 1910 ; R. E. Prothero, *The Psalms in Human Life*, 1904 (also in Nelson's Shilling Library).

THE METHOD OF STUDYING THE PSALTER

WITH SPECIAL APPLICATION TO SOME OF
THE MESSIANIC PSALMS[1]

[1] Expanded from lectures delivered at a meeting of clergy in Oxford in July, 1908, and repeated, with some additions, at a Summer School of Theology held at Oxford in September, 1909.

INTRODUCTION

IN the lectures which I have been invited to give on this subject, there is naturally much with regard to the Psalms which I must suppose to be understood and taken for granted. I cannot, for instance, describe the varied contents of the Psalter, or dwell upon its high devotional value, or explain, so far as we know them, the stages by which it gradually reached its present form. I shall only, by way of introduction, place before you a few things which we must bear in mind when we endeavour to arrive at what I conceive I was intended to help you to understand—the original meaning and purport of a few representative Psalms. I hope that the examples I shall take may place some of those who hear me in the way of applying the same method in other cases.

i. The foundation of all fruitful study of

the Psalms, as of every other part of the Old Testament, is an exact translation—resting, of course, if possible, upon a sound knowledge of the original language. But even without this independent knowledge of the original language—which all are not able to obtain—a clear and exact translation is alone often enough to teach us much : it removes many difficulties, and corrects many misunderstandings. The Prayer-book version of the Psalms, with which at least English Churchmen are most familiar, while incomparable in literary style—it was the work of Miles Coverdale, a gifted master of vigorous and idiomatic English — often, unhappily, sadly misses the sense ; and there are few Psalms in which some point or other is not in consequence seriously obscured. When we remember the date at which this version was made (1539), the existence of such blemishes is at once intelligible. What translation of what author, made nearly 400 years ago, would be adequate to the needs of the present day? It is to be regretted that the Church of England should so long

STUDYING THE PSALTER

have allowed her sons to use a version of the Psalms which constantly obscures or conceals their true meaning ; and it is matter of sincere congratulation that a motion brought forward last year in Convocation for a revision of the Prayer-book version was agreed to with great unanimity. We do not indeed want to change the *style* or *form* of our Psalter : but we do want to make it more *exact ;* and a gentle and conservative revision of the Prayer-book Psalter, which, while leaving its general style untouched, and retaining its many master-strokes of idiomatic and felicitous paraphrase, would remove its more glaring errors, and bring it into reasonable conformity with the original, is loudly called for. Inimitable as the rhythm and style of the Prayer-book version are, those who compare it carefully either with the original or with an exact translation of it, cannot be long in discovering that, if we wish to arrive at the true meaning of a Psalm, its renderings must often be discarded altogether, and new ones substituted. In pp. xl.-xlii., xlv.-vi. of my *Parallel Psalter*, I

have indicated the lines along which, as it
seems to me, a revision of the P.B. version
should be conducted. The translation in my
Parallel Psalter is based upon the Prayer-
book version, its words being preserved where-
ever possible. To preclude misunderstanding I should, however, say distinctly that it
is not designed to be a revision to supersede
it : the changes are greater than would be
necessary or desirable for that purpose :
it is intended to be read *beside* the Prayer-
book version, and to explain it. And to turn
for a few moments to the Revised Version
of the Old Testament, those who use this
version must recollect that they should never
neglect the *margins:* they must remember
that the margins have a double character ;
they are sometimes indeed inferior to the
text, but sometimes they are greatly superior
to it. As a rule, they are inferior to it, where
they merely repeat the renderings of the
Authorised Version ; they are superior to it,
where they differ from that version. To use
the Revised Version properly, the reader
should ascertain, with the help of a good

STUDYING THE PSALTER

commentary, which marginal renderings or readings are superior to those of the text, and which he may leave unnoticed. He should place a line against the former, and draw his pen or pencil through the latter.[1] It must, however, be admitted that the influence of the Authorised Version has sometimes prevented the renderings of the Revised Version from being as clear and exact as they might be ; and especially it must not be forgotten that numerous readings from the Ancient Versions, undoubtedly correct, and often both illuminative and important, are not represented in the Revised Version at all. For examples, I may refer to Professor Cheyne's *Prophecies of Isaiah* and *Book of Psalms* (ed. 1, 1888), to my own *Book of Jeremiah* in a Revised Translation (ed. 2, 1908), with short explanatory notes, to the more recent volumes of the *Cambridge Bible*, and to those of the *Century Bible*.[2]

---

[1] See more fully on this subject the Preface to my edition of *Job in the Revised Version* (Clarendon Press, 1906), pp. xxiv.-xxxiii.

[2] The reader conversant with German may also con-

THE METHOD OF

We must be prepared to accept emendations of the Massoretic text, not even excluding those based solely on conjecture. As Dr. Gray has shown recently in an interesting paper ('English Versions and the Text of the Old Testament,' in the volume of essays dedicated to Dr. Fairbairn), the older English Versions, being more or less dependent on the Vulgate, have in many passages preserved readings superior to those of later versions translated directly from the Hebrew; and, the present Hebrew text being what it is, the alternative to refusing altogether to emend it is often conjectural translation of a very improbable kind. But we must be on our guard against emending too freely or too readily: we must remember the dangers of violent or arbitrary emendation; and we must be especially cautious in seeking to force the text into conformity with a metrical or other standard which does not rest upon a perfectly sound foundation. I venture to

sult with advantage the new and enlarged edition of Kautzsch's *Die Heilige Schrift des ATs.*, with numerous exegetical as well as critical notes.

STUDYING THE PSALTER

think that the safest rule is to deviate from the Hebrew text only where the grounds are cogent, and the advantage gained is unmistakeable and clear. It is true, a large number of emendations are embraced under these conditions, but by no means so many as are necessary if we make metre our guide.[1]

[1] The Hebrew student will find an invaluable collection of various readings, in numerous cases unquestionably original, derived partly from the Ancient Versions, partly from the conjectures of modern scholars, in Kittel's *Biblia Hebraica*, 1905 (the *additions*, p. 1320 [Ed. 2, p. x.] ff., must not be neglected). The Hebrew text of this Bible is a careful reprint of that of Jacob ben Chayim in the great Rabbinical Bible published by Bomberg at Venice in 1524-5. The student should only be aware that it falls within the scope of this work to notice often various readings from the Versions, which, though in one way or another interesting, have no claim to represent the original text. The notes are in some places very numerous ; and it is interrupting and disappointing, when the reader turns to the footnote to see what the various reading is, to find one which perhaps differs from the Massoretic text only orthographically, or one which has no claim to be the original reading. To facilitate the practical use of this edition of the Hebrew Bible, the following method is strongly recommended. Let the student, when he is reading a book carefully for the first time, whether with a good com-

THE METHOD OF

ii. In order to understand the Psalms, and realise their place in the history of Israelite religion, we must, as far as we can, discover

mentary or with a teacher, put a *red* mark against the references to those various readings which he decides are practically certain, and a *blue* mark against those which he thinks are more or less probable, but does not regard as certain as those which he has marked red: when he comes afterwards to read or refer to the book again, he will see at a glance which various readings he ought to refer to, and which, for his present purpose, he can afford to disregard. In the first instance, as Kittel himself points out in a note of four pages, called 'Einige Winke über die Verwendung der Bibl. Heb. ed. Kittel im Hebräischen Unterricht' (to be obtained from the publisher, Hinrichs, Leipzig), the student would do well to confine himself to the various readings introduced by *l*. (lege, 'read').

It should be remembered that we have a measure of the corruptions that have been possible in Hebrew MSS. (1) in the Massoretic text itself, in the variations found between parallel passages (comp., e.g., Ps. xiv. with Ps. liii., Ps. xviii. with 2 Sam. xxii., Jer. lii. with 2 Kings xxiv. 18–xxv. 21, 27–30, and the margins of R.V. on Gen. xlvi. 10 ff., 1 Chron. vi. 16 ff., 34–68, xi. 27 ff., Ezr. ii. 2 ff., etc.); and (2) in the renderings of the ancient versions, especially the LXX, which presuppose texts often differing remarkably from the present Massoretic text. The Septuagint supplies cogent evidence of the strange mixture of readings, some unquestionably

STUDYING THE PSALTER

the historical situation out of which they spring. (1) The Psalms are seldom as impersonal as a modern hymn. They often describe the writer's experience ; they allude to, or even celebrate, historical events. They thus invite us, if we can, to determine the situation out of which they spring. Their dates we can only determine broadly. The criteria that we have are (*a*) the historical allusions, (*b*) the diction and literary style, (*c*) the relations to other writings whose dates are known, and (*d*) the character of the religious ideas expressed. And these rarely enable us to do more than refer a Psalm to a tolerably wide period of the history— exilic, or early or late post-exilic, for instance. Yet even this is of use, if we are interested in the growth of religious ideas, or wish to study the thought and feeling of particular ages. I can here only state briefly the conclusions, for which reasons are given in my *Introduction*. The Psalter, it is clear, assumed

superior to those of the Massoretic text, others as undeniably inferior to it, found in the Hebrew MSS. from which the Greek translation was made.

THE METHOD OF

its present form gradually, through the combination of different shorter collections by a compiler or compilers. Very few Psalms in it are earlier than the seventh century B.C., and the great majority are exilic or post-exilic. Even Book I. (Ps. i.-xli.) contains Psalms showing that it cannot have been compiled till after the exile. Of the 73 Psalms ascribed to David, internal evidence—the situation presupposed, or the ideas, or sometimes the lateness of the Hebrew—shows that certainly the greater number are of much later date.[1] The Psalter reflects the religious feelings and experiences of a long succession of pious men of Israel ; and it

---

[1] It is not to be denied that there may be a nucleus of Davidic Psalms. For an endeavour to determine some Psalms which may be Davidic, see Burney, *Interpreter*, Oct. 1909, p. 58 ff. All positive external evidence for the existence of Davidic Psalms is virtually destroyed by the untrustworthiness of the titles : where so many are demonstrably incorrect, it is clear that these, at any rate, cannot rest upon a genuine tradition. This being the case, the value of the titles generally is impaired ; and we cannot feel confident that in *any* case, they rest upon a genuine tradition.

STUDYING THE PSALTER

is no doubt to this that it owes its extraordinary variety of mood, and style, and theme. (2) Though we can seldom or never fix the actual historical occasion of a Psalm, we can often do what is of great value, reconstruct—at least in Psalms of a personal character— from the allusions and terms used, the *kind* of situation in which the poet was, and out of which the Psalm sprang. It is essential to make an effort to do this. To understand any ancient poem with topical allusions we must throw ourselves back into the position and circumstances of the writer, see with his eyes, and strive to understand how what he says is determined by the situation in which he is placed. There is great variety in the situations presupposed by the Psalms. In Psalm iii. the poet is surrounded by foes, who unite in declaring that there is no help for him in his God : but he appeals with confidence to Jehovah, who has defended him hitherto ; and foretells the discomfiture of his assailants. In Psalm iv. the writer is surrounded by impatient and distrustful companions, who blame him for some misfortune which has befallen them: he bids them regain a right frame of mind, and trust; in the joy of faith he himself can lie down and rest securely. In Psalm xi. society is in disorder. In the confusion the lives of the righteous are imperilled. The poet's despondent friends urge him to seek safety in flight: it is hopeless to attempt to stem the tide of anarchy. He replies in tones of calm and unabated confidence in Jehovah, who dwells far above the clouds which envelop the earth, and who will give the righteous their due, and speedily destroy the ungodly. The writer of Psalm xii. lives in an age of duplicity, insincerity, and untrustworthiness. By smooth words the unscrupulous threaten to get the poor into their power. The Psalmist expresses his confidence that Jehovah will deliver them. In Psalm xli. we have a most odious character presented to us. The Psalmist is ill: one who had been his intimate friend comes to visit him; he professes sympathy, but in reality is eagerly looking out for signs that he will not recover; his confederates are waiting and whispering together

STUDYING THE PSALTER

outside, hoping for the worst; he goes out and conveys to them with satisfaction the good news that the Psalmist's end is near. In Psalm xlii.–xliii.—really one Psalm, which has become accidentally divided into two —the author is somewhere in the Hermon region [' concerning ' in the Prayer-book version of xlii. 8 is a misrendering of the Latin *de*, ' from,' in Seb. Münster's Latin translation of the Old Testament, 1534–5],[1] and debarred from worshipping in the Temple; he is taunted by heathen foes with being deserted by his God. With great pathos he utters his yearnings for God, describes his dejection and distress, recalls the happiness of the past, and prays earnestly for restoration to the privileges of the sanctuary. Psalm xliv. is a national Psalm. Some great defeat has overtaken the nation; they are a scorn and derision to their neighbours. They have been true and faithful to God, and yet He has cast them off. They beseech Him to bestir Himself and save them. In Psalm lii. some wealthy and powerful noble is denounced for

[1] See my *Parallel Psalter*, p. xxii.

ruining innocent persons, and, probably, enriching himself at their expense, by malicious slanders or false evidence. His fall is confidently anticipated, while the Psalmist will be secure in the strength of his God. In Psalm lv. the poet is in great peril and mental distress. He lives among foes in a city whose walls they occupy with their patrols. He would gladly, if he could, escape to the desert. The treachery of a false friend is the bitterest ingredient in his cup of suffering. Nevertheless, in spite of the feelings of terror and indignation stirring within him, he closes with thoughts of hope and trust. Psalm lviii. is a denunciation of unjust judges. In Psalm lix. the Psalmist is in a city full of threatening and insolent foes, whose speedy fall he both prays for and expects. Psalm lx. is a prayer for victory after some great disaster. And so in other cases. We can reconstruct from the language of the Psalm the kind of situation in which its author was placed, though we cannot determine its actual writer, or the actual occasion on which it was written. It is worth bearing in mind that the characters and social conditions alluded

STUDYING THE PSALTER

to in the Psalms can often be illustrated from the prophets.

iii. A Psalm—except two or three which are evidently composite [in the case of Psalm cviii. we can demonstrate this, for it is composed of Psalm lvii. 7-11 and Psalm lx. 5-12] —is a *unity*, and must be interpreted so that its unity is preserved. The Hebrew tenses are often in themselves ambiguous. They must be rendered so that the unity of the situation is maintained. Thus the future 'shall' in the Prayer-book version of xviii. 5, 25-27, lxviii. 10, cxvi. 4, makes the Psalm incoherent. The 'is' in Psalm xxxii. 2, and the 'will' in the following verse, do the same. The principle has to be borne in mind in interpretation. We must not interpret a verse in a sense inconsistent with its context. The old atomistic style of interpretation, which often did this, must be abandoned. The Psalms are in this respect like the prophecies and the Epistles. The Bible is not a collection of disconnected dogmatic statements, any one of which may be taken, and used, regardless of its context. It is a collection of writings, each having its historical

METHOD OF STUDYING THE PSALTER

place, and each having its own unity—the unity of an historical narrative, a poem, a prophetic discourse, an epistle, as the case may be.

iv. In interpreting the Psalms, as in interpreting the other poetical books of the Old Testament and the writings of the prophets, a distinction must be drawn between the original sense and the application. The words of a Psalm may be applied to many persons and situations which were entirely out of the mind of the original writer ; and we must be careful not so to apply a Psalm as to confuse the application with the interpretation. This has a bearing on the use made of the Psalms in the New Testament, and also by the Church (to which I shall revert later) ; and to avoid confusion and mistake it is important to bear it in mind.

PSALM II

PSALM II

LET us then consider Psalm ii. and see whether it is possible to reconstruct the historical situation presupposed by it.

The Psalm is artistically constructed, and falls into four strophes of nearly equal length ; it also displays great poetical vigour and dramatic power. Its central thought is the world-wide dominion of the King of Zion.[1]

First strophe (*vv.* 1-3). The poet begins by describing a confederacy of subject nations, mustering for a revolt, and eager to cast off their allegiance to the theocratic king of Israel :—

1 Why do the nations throng tumultuously,[2]

---

[1] The notes are not intended to be exhaustive, but merely to explain or illustrate points of interest.

[2] The root is rare in Heb. (only the subst. *throng* twice besides, Ps. lv. 14, lxiv. 2 [see R.V. m.] ; but the meaning is clear from Aramaic ; see Dan. vi. 6, 11, 15 (R.V.m.).

and the peoples meditate [1] emptiness ?
2 The kings of the earth take their stand,
   and the rulers sit in conclave [2] together,
   against Jehovah and against his anointed (saying) :
3 'Let us knap their thongs in sunder,
   and fling away their cords from us.'

The scene in *vv*. 1, 2 is presented with dramatic vividness ; we see the actors all in movement before us (the Hebrew student will notice the imperfect tenses in *vv*. 1*b*, 2*a*). The 'thongs' are the thongs of the yoke, which, in the case of a literal yoke, bound it round the animal's neck (see Jer. v. 5 ; xxvii. 2). Before *v*. 3 we must, as often in Hebrew poetry, supply in thought, '(saying)' : instead of describing what the kings and rulers do, the poet, more graphically and dramatically,

---

In the Targums the verb is often used for the Heb. המה (e.g. Ps. xlvi. 6*a*). (Where the Hebrew and English verse-numbers differ, as they often do in the Psalms,—the titles, if long, being counted as *v*. 1 in the Heb.),—the references here and in the sequel are always to the *English*.)

[1] Properly, *murmur* or *mutter*. So always.
[2] Or, changing one letter, *assemble themselves*. See the note.

STUDYING THE PSALTER

represents them as declaring defiantly what they intend. In English, in such cases, to make the meaning clear, we should use naturally inverted commas.

In *v.* 2 'sit in conclave' is in Heb. נוסדו —in this sense only Ps. xxxi. 13 [Heb. 14] besides. Elsewhere the verb always means to *found* (Ps. xxiv. 2). Perhaps the primary idea of the root was to *fix firm* or *close*, usually taken in the sense of *to found*, but also having in Nifal, in the reflexive sense of the conjugation, the meaning *fix* or *seat themselves close together*, i.e. 'sit in conclave.' But Lagarde's נועדו, *meet by appointment*, *assembled themselves* (Ps. xlviii. 4 [5]; and esp. Neh. vi. 2), is a very probable emendation. As Dr. Gray has recently pointed out (in the paper cited above, p. 23), to adopt a conjectural *emendation* of the Hebrew text— provided it be not a violent one—is not more arbitrary or venturesome than to assign a conjectural *meaning* to a Hebrew word. To treat יסד here as a denom. from סוד, or as a parallel form of סוד, and to render *confer* or *consult together* (Duhm, Bäthgen, *al.*), is precarious. It is true, סוד, like $s^ew\bar{o}d$ in Syriac, means properly *intimate* or *friendly converse* (see my note on Am. iii. 7 in the *Cambridge Bible*); but no verb סוד is found in the Old Testament, its first and, seemingly, its only occurrence being Ecclus. vii. 14 (Heb.); in Syriac the form regularly used is the reflexive ܐܣܬܘܕ (so אֶסְתַּיַּד or אָסְתּוּד in the Aramäising Hebrew of Ecclus. viii. 17; ix. 3, 14; xlii. 12). Where there is so little evidence that סוד was a genuine Hebrew verb, it is hazardous to assume, on the strength of Ges.-K. §§ 77c, 78b, a parallel form to it, יסד.

Second strophe (*vv*. 4–6). Jehovah mocks from heaven their puny efforts ; His king is firmly established upon Zion.

> 4 He that sitteth in heaven laugheth :
> the Lord mocketh at them.
> 5 Then shall he speak unto them in his anger,
> and dismay them in his hot displeasure :
> 6 'But *I* have installed[1] my king
> upon Zion, my holy mountain.'

---

[1] Elsewhere in this sense only Prov. viii. 23. The Heb. verb *nāsakh* in all other passages means to *pour out* a libation (Ps. xvi. 4, etc.), or, of molten metal, to *cast* (Is. xl. 19 ; cf. the derivative *massēkhāh*, a *molten* image) ; hence, in default of any better explanation, it used generally to be supposed either that to *pour out* in these passages meant to *anoint*, or, as cast metal becomes afterwards solid and firm, that the verb had acquired the secondary sense of *fix* or *set firm*. Neither of these explanations was, however, satisfactory. It is now known (Delitzsch, *Ass. H.W.B.*, p. 472) that there is an Assyrian verb, *nasâku*, used of *setting up*, or *installing*, a king, with a deriv. *nasiku*, *prince*, corresponding to the Heb. נסיך, *prince* (Ps. lxxxiii. 11 *al.*). It can hardly be doubted that the Hebrew verb, as used in Ps. ii. 6 and Prov. viii. 23, is to be explained from this Assyrian

STUDYING THE PSALTER

He that sitteth (viz. enthroned, which is often the implication of the word : see e.g. xxix. 10, lv. 19) *in heaven* is a title in finely-conceived contrast to the inhabitants of earth, vainly plotting to thwart His purpose. For the anthropomorphism *mocketh*, cf. Psalm lix. 8. Before *v.* 6 we must again supply in thought, '(saying).'

Third strophe (*vv.* 7–9). The king is here suddenly introduced speaking, and reciting the Divine decree of sonship which gives him authority over the nations of the earth. This assures him of his position, and gives him confidence.

7 I will tell concerning the decree :
    Jehovah said unto me, ' Thou art my son ;
    ' *I* have this day begotten thee :
8 ' Ask of me, and I will give the nations for thine inheritance,
    ' and the ends of the earth for thy possession :

---

word. There must have been in Hebrew—as analogously in many other cases—two distinct roots, *nāsakh*,—one, occurring frequently, meaning to *pour out*, and the other, preserved only in two places, meaning to *set up*, *instal*, with the derivative נסיך, *prince*, properly one *installed* into some dignity.

9 'Thou shalt break them with a mace[1] of iron;
   'thou shalt dash them in pieces like a potter's vessel.'

In *v.* 7 ('I will tell') the speaker is the king; there are in Hebrew poetry many similar cases, in which the speaker has to be inferred from the context. The 'decree' is the promise given by Nathan to David (2 Sam. vii. 12–14): [12] 'When thy days are fulfilled, and thou shalt sleep with thy fathers, I will set up thy seed after thee, which shall proceed out of thy bowels, and I will establish his kingdom. [13] He shall build an house for my name, and I will establish the throne of his kingdom for ever. [14] *I will be to him a father, and he shall be to me a son: if he* commit iniquity, I will chasten him with the rod of men, and with the stripes of the children of men (i.e. as human fathers are wont to correct their children,—as far as may be necessary, yet not so far as to cast them off); [15] but my kindness shall not depart from him, as I took it from Saul,

---

[1] The 'spiked iron mace used in war' (Cheyne). Or, *sceptre* (fig. for *rule*), as Ps. xlv. 6.

whom I put away from before thee. ¹⁶ And thine house and thy kingdom shall be made sure for ever before me (so LXX); thy throne shall be established for ever ' (compare the poetical amplification of the passage in Psalm lxxxix. 26-37). In the original promise, it will be noticed, the words refer either to Solomon, or, as the word ' seed ' in $v.$ 13 and the context generally suggest, the Davidic dynasty in general (in which case $v.$ 13 will be a later gloss [1]); in either case the possibility of the ruler spoken of *sinning* is expressly contemplated ($v.$ 14b). In Psalm ii., however, the poet takes the promise of $v.$ 14a absolutely, and leaves this possibility out of the question. ' Thou art my son ' was perhaps (Gunkel)[2] a formula of adoption : hitherto the king has had only a human father ; now he is to have a Divine father. ' *I* have this day begotten thee ' expands and enforces ' Thou art my son ' ; the ' day ' is

[1] See Kennedy's note on the passage in the *Century Bible*.

[2] *Ausgewählte Psalmen übersetzt und erklärt* (1904), p. 12.

the one on which the king had been anointed, and formally installed into his kingly rights. This august title had been conferred upon him then.

It ought to be remembered that the figures applied here to the king are used elsewhere of the *nation*. Thus Israel was figuratively Jehovah's 'son,' his 'firstborn' (Exod. iv. 22 ; Hos. xi. 1)—the relation being conceived, not, as was often the case among heathen nations, as a physical one, but as a *moral* one, implying on the one side fatherly affection and care, and on the other filial devotion and obedience.[1] Even the same word 'begotten' is used of the nation, Deut. xxxii. 18 : ' Of the Rock that *begat* thee thou wast unmindful, and forgattest God that was in travail with thee.' There, however, the word is used as a figure for the origin of the nation ; here it is a figure for the king's installation into the rights of sonship.

Vv. 8–9. Inheritance is the natural right

---

[1] Cf. Isa. i. 2 (of individual Israelites), and see more fully my *Deuteronomy*, pp. 156 (on xiv. 1), and 352 (on xxxii. 5).

STUDYING THE PSALTER

of sonship; and as Jehovah's adopted son, the king here spoken of has but to ask his Father, and He will give him the whole earth as his possession; if any of his subjects presume to revolt, he will bring upon them complete and irreparable destruction.

For *break them*, the **LXX**, pronouncing תְּרְעֵם for תְּרֹעֵם has 'thou shalt *shepherd* them' ($\pi οιμανεῖς\ αὐτοὺς$—fig. for *rule*, as 2 Sam. v. 2; Ps. lxxviii. 72 *al.* [**R.V.** *feed*]), and this is the source of to 'shepherd the nations with a rod of iron' in Revelation ii. 27, xii. 5, xix. 15; but the parallel *dash to pieces* supports the Massoretic vocalisation 'shalt *break* them.'

Strophe 4 (*vv.* 10–12). The poet speaks, drawing the practical lesson from Jehovah's words. Let the nations yield willing submission to Jehovah's son, instead of resisting to their own destruction.

10 Now, therefore, O ye kings, be wise;
    be admonished, ye judges of the earth.
11 Serve Jehovah with fear,
    and rejoice with trembling.

THE METHOD OF [PSALM

12 Kiss the son, lest he be angry, and ye perish as regards
the way ;
for his anger burneth quickly :
happy are all they that take refuge in him.

V. 10. *Be admonished;* **properly,** *Let yourselves be admonished* (the *Nifal tolerativum*, **Ges.-K.** § 51c). Cf. the same word, addressed to Jerusalem, in Jer. vi. 8. Notice that in P.B.V. *be learned* is a euphemism for *be taught*, according to an old usage of ' learn ' (so lxxxii. 5 ' They will not be *learned*,' i.e. be *taught;* xxv. 4 ' Lead me forth in thy truth and *learn* me), still current among the poorer classes, and dialectically.

V. 11. It is possible that for יִגְּלוּ, *rejoice*, we should read חִילוּ, ' Be in awe ' (see Ps. xcvi. 9, cxiv. 7 [R.V. *tremble*]). It is true, of course, that in the attitude of a religious man towards his God joy and fear are no incompatible emotions : but regard must be had to the context ; and it seems more likely that insurgent rebels would be exhorted to be in awe than to rejoice. *Reverence* (P.B.V.) in the next line is incorrect : רְעָדָה denotes never religious fear, but always *alarm* or *trembling:* see Ps. xlviii. 6, xxxiii. 14, Job iv. 14 ; רַעַד Ps. lv. 5, Exod. xv. 15 ; and the verb in Ps. civ. 32.

V. 12. *Kiss the son*, the ' son ' spoken of

above, the Israelitish king : pay him the homage that is his due, lest He (i.e. Jehovah) be angry with you for resisting the king who is His ' son,' and His wrath kindle against you with destructive force. The kiss is a figure for homage and regard (1 Sam. x. 1 ; 1 Kings xix. 18 ; Hosea xiii. 2 ; Job xxxi. 2— in the last three passages, paid to a deity). The Aramaic *bar* (elsewhere in Hebrew only three times in the late passage, Prov. xxxi. 2) is strange, especially as we have the Hebrew *ben* in *v.* 7 ; but it would be accounted for if the Psalm were late ; and it is difficult to find a more satisfactory rendering ; nor are the emendations that have been proposed convincing. We must admit the uncertainty of the passage, but happily it does not affect the general sense of the Psalm : as the sequel shows, there must have stood here, however it may have been expressed, some admonition to submit to either Jehovah or His king.

The chief other renderings are (1) LXX δράξασθε παιδείας ' Lay hold of instruction ' ; hence Jerome in the Vulg. *apprehendite disciplinam* ; Targ. קבילו אולפנא,

'receive the teaching.' The origin of this rendering is uncertain; it *may* imply a different reading (מוּסָר —cognate with the verb rendered 'be admonished' in *v.* 7 or מוּ. בַר, having dropped out after the קוּ of נשׁקוּ, and סר having become corrupted into בַר); it *may* depend on a Midrashic explanation of בַר, as signifying the 'law.'[1] The meaning *lay hold of* for נשׁק is also very uncertain. (*a*) The corresponding word in Arabic, *nasaḳa*, means to *arrange together in order*, as pearls on a string, or a discourse (cf. *sermo* from *serere*); (*b*) in Hebrew it occurs three times with some such idea as *handling* a bow (Ps. lxxviii. 9; 1 Chron. xii. 2), or a bow and shield (2 Chron. xvii. 17); but exactly *what* idea it denotes in this connexion can only be conjectured; (*c*) then, further, the cognate *nēshek̠* denotes a *weapon*, or, collectively, *armour* (Job xx. 24. Ezek. xxxix. 9; 1 Kings x. 25, 2 Kings x. 12); but again, what the etymological meaning of the word is, is quite uncertain. Thus the rendering *lay hold of* rests upon a very insecure philological foundation; it would no

---

[1] Some of the Rabbis interpreted *bar*, 'corn,' in Prov. xi. 26, as a figure for the *law* (*Sanh.* 92*a* : in Wünsche's transl., *Der Bab. Talm. in seinen Haggadischen Bestandtheilen übersetzt*, II. iii., 1889, p. 154 f.); and they understood Ps. ii. 11 in the same sense, 'Kiss the corn of the law!' (*ibid.*; Midrash *Tehillin*, on Ps. ii. 11, in Wünsche's transl., p. 30; Midrash *Mishlê* on xi. 26), and even Prov. xxxi. 2 (Midrash *Bemidbar Ra^bba*, on Num. vi. 2; in Wünsche's tr., p. 214).

STUDYING THE PSALTER

doubt suit (*b*) if this stood by itself, but it is difficult to connect with (*a*) and (*c*).

(2) Hitzig rendered *Lay hold of* (or *embrace*) *obedience* (cf. Kirkpatrick, in the *Cambridge Bible*, p. 12, ' or, perhaps, *obedience* '), deriving *bar* from the Arab. *barra*, to be *pious* towards God, *dutiful* towards parents, *kind* towards others, whence *bir*, *piety*, *dutifulness*, and *kindness*, and especially *obedience* towards God (Lane, *Arab. Lex.*, pp. 175, 176*c*). But apart from the doubtful rendering *Lay hold of*, *th*e strong Arabism is not probable.

(3) Aquila rendered καταφιλήσατε ἐκλεκτῶς (cf. Cant. vi. 9), and Symmachus προςκυνήσατε καθαρῶς (cf. Job xi. 4), whence Jerome, in his own translation from the Hebrew, *adorate pure*—all taking בר as an adv. (cf. מר יבכיון, Isa. xxxiii. 7) ; so Dr. Briggs, only vocalising בֹּר, and construing as an adv. accusative, ' kiss in purity '—let your homage be unsullied by any secret blemish (Job xxxi. 27 f.). This construction is quite grammatical (cf. אהבם נדבה, Hos. xiv. 4 [5], Ges.-K. § 118*q*) ; but both *bar*, *clean* or *pure*, and *bōr*, *cleanness*, *purity*, are rare (Job xi. 4, and of the heart Ps. xix. 8, xxiv. 4, lxxiii. 1 ; of the hands Ps. xviii. 20, 24, Job xxii. 30) ; and one rather wonders whether either is a likely word to have been used here. Still, the rendering is certainly more probable than either (1) or (2). It is remarkable that none of the Ancient Versions, except the Syriac, should have given what seems to be the most natural rendering of the Hebrew, *Kiss the son*, not even Aq., Symm. and Jerome, though they plainly had before them the same consonantal text which we have, and though, too, the explanation of a Hebrew word from

the Aramaic is anything but uncommon in the versions, especially in the LXX. Jerome mentions the rendering *Kiss the son*, but seems to think it scarcely worth considering: his words are 'Pro eo quod in Graeco dicitur δράξασθε παιδείας, in Hebraeo legitur NESCU BAR, quod interpretari potest, *adorate filium*.'

(4) Lagarde (*Novae Psalterii graeci editionis specimen*, 1887, p. 24 f.), assuming that the LXX really read מוּסָר, argues in favour of adopting these consonants, but vocalising them differently, and adding a suffix, would read מוֹסְרוֹ [or, better, מוֹסֵרוֹ], i.e., '*Lay hold of his thongs*' (so Cheyne, *Origin of the Psalter*, p. 351, 'Put on (again) his bonds'[1]): נָשֵׁק, 'lay hold of,' in *v*. 12 would then, he points out, form an effective alliterative antithesis to נִתֵּק, 'knap in sunder' in *v*. 3. But 'lay hold of,' even if (see above) it were certainly the meaning of נשק, does not seem to be quite the idea that we should expect in connexion with 'thongs.'

(5) It has often been remarked (cf. the note above) that 'rejoice' in *v*. 11 agrees indifferently with 'trembling': and Professor Bertholet, of Bâle, has made recently (*Z. für alttest. Wiss.*, 1908, p. 58 f.) an ingenious suggestion for removing at one stroke both this incongruity and the troublesome *bar*. He suggests viz. that two words have been accidentally transposed: the original text being

ונשקו ברגלו ברעדה [2]

---

[1] Discarded in *Psalms*, ed. 2 (1904), in favour of a different conjecture.

[2] In the autographs, and early copies, of the Old

A scribe, he supposes, accidentally omitted the second to the seventh letters from the right, which he added afterwards at the end, thus producing

ונלו ברעדה נשקו בר

We should then get for the original form of the verse—

> 11. Serve Jehovah with fear.
>   and *kiss his feet* with trembling ;
> 12. Lest he be angry, and ye perish, etc.

And he points out that to 'kiss the feet' is a common expression in Assyrian, used both of submission to a conqueror, and also in particular of homage to a deity.[1] Bertholet afterwards found that he had been partly anticipated in his conjecture, both by Sievers (*ibid.* p.

Testament writings, the divisions between words must have been often imperfectly marked, even if they were marked at all (they are often not marked in inscriptions) : the renderings of the LXX often presuppose a division of words different from that in the present Massoretic text ; and in the Massoretic text itself there are undoubted instances of words incorrectly divided (in Gen. xlix. 19–20, for instance, we must certainly read אשר עקבם for עקב מאשר, in 2 Sam. xxi. 1 ואל ביתה דמים for ואל בית הדמים and in Hos. vi. 5 ומשפטי כאור יצא for ומשפטיך אור. See further examples in my *Notes on Samuel*, p. xxxi. f.

[1] Bertholet cites, for examples, Jastrow, *Die Relig. Bab. u. Ass.* i. 514, ii. 103, and Delitzsch, *H.W.B.* p. 486*b*.

193), and by the learned Dominican scholar, Père Lagrange (*Revue Bibl.*, 1905, p. 40, cited *ibid.* p. 234). It is an objection to Bertholet's suggestion, not met by the parallels cited by him (נגע, דבק, אחז, construed with ב), that נשק is construed often with ל (as well as with an accus.), but never with ב. Still it is possible that ברגלו itself, in the MS. which was copied incorrectly, might be an error for an earlier לרגלו. Even so, however, to 'kiss the feet' is an expression not elsewhere found in Hebrew; and though the feet of Marduk or a goddess might be kissed by a worshipper in Assyria, it may be doubted whether such an anthropomorphism would be used by a worshipper of Yahweh in Israel. There seems also to be no apparent reason, such as an ὁμοιοτέλευτον, to explain the scribe's supposed error. The case is one in which, while the traditional text, and generally accepted rendering, are not above suspicion, the alternative renderings or readings proposed are not free from objection.

The Psalmist ends by congratulating those who place themselves under Jehovah's protection, by accepting the rule of His king. The rendering of P.B.V., A.V. and R.V. ' put their trust in him ' obliterates the suggestive figure of the original, which is that of *taking refuge* or *shelter*. The same figure is often obliterated elsewhere : see the passages cited in the Glossary to my *Parallel Psalter*, under *refuge*, p. 454. The expression, when referred to Jehovah, always implies trustful confidence ; but the sense of the figure is often consciously felt, and it is a loss to confuse the word with the ordinary word for *trust*. Comp. Jud. ix. 15, where the bramble says to the other trees, ' Come and *take refuge* in my shadow,' Isa. xxx. 2, 3 ' to *take refuge* in the shadow of Egypt,' Ruth ii. 12 ' under whose wings thou art come—not to ' trust ' but— to *take refuge* ' (so here R.V.). In Psalms xxxvi. 7, lvii. 1, lxi. 4, xci. 4 (in all with ' wings ') R.V. also has rightly *take refuge*. Comp. the cognate subst. מחסה, regularly rendered *refuge*—in Isaiah iv. 6 from a storm, and often figuratively of Jehovah (Ps. xiv. 6, xlvi. 1, etc., and expressly from a storm, Isa. xxv. 4).

Is it possible to determine the occasion of the Psalm ? Insurrections in the reigns of David or Solomon have been suggested : but though these kings had their foes, there is no mention or probability of a revolt of subject-nations from either of them, such as is here depicted. We might think better of a

later king, when some of Israel's neighbours—
Edom, Moab, or Ammon—subdued by David
(2 Sam. viii.) may have assailed Judah ; and
this may have been painted by the poet as
a revolt of subject-nations generally, the
actual occasion being magnified and made the
basis of an ideal description of the triumph of
Jehovah and His king. It is very possible,
however, that Bäthgen is right in regarding
the whole representation as ideal : the prophets had spoken of the assaults of nations
upon Israel, and of their defeat—sometimes of
actual assaults, as of the Assyrians, Isaiah
xvii. 12–14, sometimes of imaginary ones,
like that of Magog, whom Ezekiel (ch.
xxxviii., xxxix.) represents as advancing against
the restored Israel only to be annihilated by
Divine intervention (xxxviii. 21 f.) ; they had
proclaimed Israel's supremacy over other
nations ; they had also drawn the picture of
Israel's ideal king, and of his victories over
his foes. On the basis of these representations
there had grown up the idea, current in
apocalyptic writings, of the advent of an age
when the heathen who held Israel enthralled

would be subdued, and when Israel would rule in freedom and glory over the world. The Psalmist does not give the reins to his imagination as these writers do ; but he is moving on the same lines. ' He lived in an age when Israel was surrounded by powerful foes ; but he was also inspired by strong religious and national feeling ' (Bäthgen). On the basis of older prophecies of the rule of the ideal king, combined with reminiscences of the rule of David and Solomon, and the promise of Nathan in 2 Samuel vii. 14, the poet constructs an imaginative picture of his rule established over all the earth, of the nations and their kings revolting, of their failure, and of the re-establishment by Jehovah of the rule of His ideal king (so Bäthgen). This view is attractive : whether it is correct, is more than we can say. If it is, the Psalm will contain a poetical representation of world-wide empire conferred by Jehovah upon the ideal ruler of the future, and solemnly confirmed to him by Him. If *bar* in *v*. 12 is correct, and means ' son,' the Psalm is almost certainly post-exilic ; the Aram. רגשׁ

in *v.* 1 points in the same direction : and it is to the post-exilic age—perhaps early in the Greek period, when Syrians and Egyptians were contending for the possession of Coele-Syria and Palestine—that, if the Psalm is rightly interpreted in the last-mentioned sense, it will most naturally be assigned.

The Psalm is thus, if the 'king' spoken of in it is an actual king of Israel, 'typically' Messianic, i.e. it invests the actual king, and his rule, with such ideal features as to make him typical of a future *ideal* king: if the 'king,' in accordance with the last suggestion, is the future ideal ruler of Israel, it will be directly Messianic. 'Messiah'—properly מלכא משיחא, '*the* anointed king,' κατ' ἐξοχήν —was the name given by the later Jews to the ideal ruler, whose figure they constructed on the basis of representations in the Old Testament, and who they believed would one day appear to deliver them from the tyranny of the nations, and assume the rule of the world[1] : stripped of its worldly features,

---

[1] Comp. e.g. in the so-called 'Psalms of Solomon' (written probably *c.* 70 B.C.), where there is a prayer to

STUDYING THE PSALTER

and spiritualised, the ideal was appropriated and realised by Jesus. In either case, the Psalm is 'Messianic' not by being a direct prediction, but through its describing an *ideal* rule, which, in a larger and more spiritual sense than the Psalmist's words actually suggest, was fulfilled by Christ. And so the Psalm is quoted, more than once, in the New Testament, with reference to Christ. Verses 1 and 2 are quoted by St. Peter in Acts iv. 20 f.—not indeed as a *prediction*, for there was then no rebellion of subject-nations against a king, such as the Psalm depicts (notice *v*. 3), but—as describing a hostility, *exemplified* then, in a signal manner, by the Jews and Gentiles confederate against Him. In Acts xiii. 33, *v*. 7 ('Thou art my son,' etc.) is quoted as testifying to the truth of Christ's resurrection : again, not as a prediction,

God that He will 'raise up to them their king, the son of David,' who will 'destroy the ungodly nations with the word of his mouth,' and 'gather together a holy people' round himself in Jerusalem, whom he will 'lead in righteousness,' while he will 'possess the nations of the heathen to serve him beneath his yoke' (xvii. 23, 27, 28, 32). See in Ryle and James' edition, p. 137 ff.

because, as has been shown, the words relate in reality to something entirely different, but because the resurrection of Jesus was a signal testimony to His being in the fullest sense of the word (and not only as the Psalmist took it) the 'son' of God, and the true 'Messiah.' Psalm ii. is accordingly read appropriately in the Anglican Church on Easter-day. And in Hebrews i. 5, the same verse, together with 2 Samuel vii. 14a,[1] is quoted as showing Christ's superiority to the angels : no angel had ever been addressed in terms such as those used in these two passages. But again it must be recognised that the apostle understands the words in a higher and larger sense than that which they actually bear in the Old Testament itself : in the case of the Psalm this follows from what has been said above in the note on the verse ; and it is, if possible, even clearer in the case of 2 Samuel vii. 14a ; for there, as the context shows (v. 14b ; see p.

---

[1] Compare Rom. i. 4 *marked out* as the son of God with power . . . by the resurrection of the dead ' (meaning His resurrection ; see Sanday and Headlam on the sense of the Greek expression used).

32), the term 'father' cannot be used in a loftier sense than that in which it might be used in relation to a 'son,' the possibility of whose sinning is expressly contemplated by the writer.[1] As we proceed we shall meet with other illustrations of the varied use made of Old Testament passages in the New Testament. But our method of dealing with them must in all cases be the same : as in all exegesis, our first duty must be to discover, as accurately as we can, the exact picture, or idea, which the Old Testament writer means his reader to form ; when we have done this, we shall be in a position to appreciate rightly the manner in which it is applied in the New Testament.

---

[1] Comp. Westcott, *Epistle to the Hebrews*, p. 19 : 'The whole passage (2 Sam. vii. 14), with its reference to "iniquity" and chastening, can only refer to an earthly king; and still experience showed that no earthly king could satisfy its terms. The kingdom passed away from the line of David.' It was necessary, therefore, to look for another 'seed,' of whom its terms should be true without reservation (*v.* 14*b*) or restriction.

PSALM XLV

PSALM XLV

THE occasion of this Psalm is evidently a royal marriage. The poet—as a modern poet among ourselves might do—puts into tuneful words the feelings of national pride and satisfaction befitting the occasion : he celebrates in glowing terms the graces and felicity of the bridegroom, the splendour of the queen, and anticipates for him a glorious and successful reign. The hopes to which the auspicious occasion gives rise are analogous to those which we find elsewhere in psalms or prophecies relating to the king ; they differ only in so far as the occasion which evokes them is a marriage. We do not know either who the poet is, or whose nuptials he celebrates : verse 10*b*, if not verse 12, seems to imply that the bride is a foreigner ; and so the marriage of Solomon with Pharaoh's daughter, or of Jehoram of Judah with Athaliah, the daughter of Ahab and Jezebel, have been thought of. Happily we can understand the Psalm without knowing what the specific occasion is which it celebrates. We must only make an effort to transport ourselves from our own days to those of ancient Jerusalem—or, it may be, of Samaria—and picture in one of these ancient capitals of Israel a gala day—the people elated with enthusiasm and excitement, full of joyous anticipations, greeting their king and his bride with bright auguries and warm congratulations.

1 My heart is astir[1] with a goodly matter ;
    I will say[2] that which I have written[3] unto the
        king :
    my tongue is the pen of a ready writer—

---

[1] *Rāḥash* occurs only here in the Old Testament : it does not mean to *overflow* (R.V.), but *to keep moving, be astir* (see the *Oxf. Heb. Lex.*, p. 935*b*, with the references).

[2] Lit. *I am saying*, i.e. *I am about to say or will say ;* cf. Genesis xix. 13 ' we will destroy this place ' (lit. *are destroying*), 1 Samuel xii. 16 ' which Jehovah will do before your eyes ' (lit. *is doing*). See my *Hebrew Tenses*, § 135, 3 ; or G.-K. § 116*p*.

[3] Lit. *my work*, i.e. my composition (cf. Engl. *work*, of a book ; and ποίημα, a ' poem '). In the translation ' my

and quick, therefore, to express the inspiring thoughts stirring in his heart. Forthwith he proceeds to describe the high qualities of the royal bridegroom—his personal beauty, the winsome smile upon his lips, witnessing to the gracious words that he can speak, and the gracious qualities, befitting a noble-minded monarch, which he possesses; and showing that he deserves, therefore, that God's blessing should rest continuously upon him—

> 2 Thou art fairer than the children of men:
> graciousness is shed over thy lips:
> therefore God hath blessed thee for ever.

He is, moreover, a warrior, ready—as the Israelite kings ever were—to lead his army into battle and bravely wrestle with his foes; so the poet bids him equip himself in martial majesty and state, and use his weapons in the cause of truth and right—

---

work' is avoided, as a poor and prosaic expression; and a rendering adapted from the P.B.V. has been adopted.

THE METHOD OF   [PSALM

3 Gird thy sword upon thy thigh, O mighty one,[1]
   (even) thy majesty and thy state.
4 [2]And (in) thy state, [5]ride on, press through,[3]
   on behalf of faithfulness, and humility, (and) right-
      eousness :
   and may thy right hand teach thee terrible things !

not (P.B.V.) ' because of the *word* of truth,' etc., but ' *on behalf,*' i.e. ' *in the cause of* faithfulness,' etc., in defence of virtues which are trampled under foot in evil times and under evil rulers, but which a just ruler would do his utmost to foster and promote. He is ' to protect the faithful as opposed to liars and deceivers, the righteous as opposed to breakers of the law, and the humble as opposed to the proud ' (Cheyne). We remember how David and Solomon ' executed judgement and justice ' in the land (2 Sam. viii. 15, 1 Kings

---

[1] I.e. *O warrior*, according to the standing meaning of *gibbōr*, ' mighty one,' as in David's ' mighty men ' (2 Sam. xxi. 8, etc.).

[2] The repetition of exactly the same word (הדרך) that occurs at the end of *v.* 3, and the harshness of the construction in this verse, render the text very suspicious : but no convincing emendation has been proposed.

[3] Or, *prosper* (Jer. xxii. 20).

x. 9), how often the defenceless and, especially, the godly poor were oppressed in Israel, and how to do justice and to help and protect the oppressed is mentioned, both in the prophets, and in other Psalms, as an attribute of the ideal ruler (Isa. ix. 7, xvi. 5; Jer. xxiii. 5; Isa. xi. 4, xxxii. 2; Ps. lxxii. 4, 12–14). May his right hand, the poet adds, teach him to do terrible things! i.e., may his courage show him how to do acts of terrible valour in defence of this great cause!

> 5 Thine arrows are sharpened;
>   peoples fall under thee;
>   (they are) in the heart of the king's enemies.

His arrows are sharp, ready to be aimed with fatal effect: his enemies fall before him, and he rides over their prostrate corpses (cf. Ps. xviii. 38 'I smite them through that they cannot rise: they fall under my feet'); each shaft has penetrated the heart of a foe.

The Psalmist continues—

> 6 Thy throne, O God, is for ever and ever:
>   a sceptre of equity is the sceptre of thy kingdom.

It is evident that the words are addressed

to the king whose nobility and prowess the poet is celebrating. The words cannot, as from Hebrews i. 8 onwards has often been supposed, be an affirmation of the divinity of the Messiah, for the simple reason that the king whom the psalmist celebrates, though he is invested with ideal attributes, is not the Messiah—least of all the Christian Messiah, for he marries a queen and has children, who are spoken of in such terms that it would outrage all reasonable exegesis to understand them in any but a literal sense. Nor can we rend the Psalm in two, and apply the rest of the Psalm to the Israelite king, and this one verse to the Messiah. Thus, not upon theological, but upon *exegetical* grounds, the current interpretation of the passage cannot be sustained. Gressmann,[1] accepting the correctness of the text, supposes that the use of the term 'God' is a survival from a time when the Israelite king was regarded as divine and addressed as God. But that cannot be said to be probable. The rendering of R.V.m.

[1] *Ursprung der Isr.-jüdischen Eschatologie* (1905), p. 256 f.

would remove the difficulty ; but it is questionable philologically.[1] If, however, with a very slight change of text, we might suppose, with Mr. Edghill,[2] that a *kaph*, written properly twice, had been transcribed only once, we should at once obtain a suitable sense : ' Thy throne is *as* God '—i.e. by Hebrew idiom, ' as God's throne ' (cf. Ps. xviii. 33 ' who maketh my feet like hinds,' i.e., of course, not like the hinds themselves, but ' like hinds' feet ' ; and see G.-K. § 141*d*, *note*). This appears to be the best suggestion for the explanation of the text that has been made : the textual change is slight, and the sense obtained is in excellent agreement with the context. The king's throne, it is said hyperbolically, is to be as permanent as God's throne : (cf. xxi. 4, where the king is said to have been given ' length of days for ever and ever (עולם ועד),' and lxi. 6, 7 ' Days mayest thou add to the days of the king ! May his years be as many generations ! May he

---

[1] See my *Hebrew Tenses*, § 194 *Obs*.

[2] *An Enquiry into the Evidential Value of Prophecy* (1906), p. 252.

sit (enthroned) before God for ever (עולם) ! '
And his rule is to be one of equity : ' A sceptre
of equity is the sceptre of thy kingdom.' A
rule of equity was always one of the first
traits which the Israelite drew in his portrait
of an ideal king (cf. Isa. xi. 4, 5, Jer. xxiii. 5,
Ps. lxxii. 2, and elsewhere). And the poet
views the king's present good fortune as the
reward of his high moral attributes :—

> 7 Thou lovest righteousness, and hatest iniquity :
> therefore God, thy God, hath anointed thee
> with the oil of gladness above thy fellows.

The point in the last clause is not the anointing but the gladness : the anointing and the oil are both meant figuratively, the expression ' oil of gladness,' as in Isaiah lxi. 3, being suggested by the ancient custom of anointing with oil on festal occasions (Ps. civ. 15 ; Am. vi. 6 ; Luke vii. 46) ; the meaning is thus, not that he has been literally anointed, but that he has been made happier than other kings by his present auspicious marriage.

> 8 All thy garments are myrrh, and aloes, (and) cassia ;
> out of ivory palaces stringed instruments make thee
> glad.

STUDYING THE PSALTER

9 King's daughters are among thy precious ones :
  upon thy right hand standeth the consort[1] in gold
    of Ophir.

V. 8 describes the king as he appears arrayed for the occasion ; his garments are scented with costly perfumes fetched from distant lands ; [2] as he approaches his palace, inlaid, like Ahab's, with ivory, the sounds of music greet him. *V.* 9, *kings*' daughters—so splendid is his court—are among the inmates of his harem—for that is the meaning of the

---

[1] Not the usual word for *queen*. Elsewhere only Neh. ii. 6, Dan. v. 2, 3, 23 ('wives') ; and read by some scholars conjecturally in Judges v. 30 *end* ('for the neck of the *consort*').

[2] *Myrrh* was brought from Arabia. *Aloes* (Heb. *ăhā-lōth*) is the Greek ἀγάλλοχον, the modern 'eagle-wood' (from the Malay *agil*), an aromatic wood, exported from India and Ceylon, which, when burnt, yields a fragrant odour. It is quite different from the bitter medicine which we call *aloes* (Gk. ἀλόη). The fragrant aloes are mentioned also in Cant. iv. 14, Proverbs vii. 17—in both places joined with 'myrrh.' *Cassia*—here lit. *scrapings* (the word in Exodus xxx. 24, Ezekiel xxvii. 19 is different), used specifically of the scrapings, or powder, of a fragrant bark—is the powdered bark of (probably) a species of cinnamon, indigenous in South India and Malacca (see *Enc. Bibl.*, i. 708).

'honourable'[1] women of the English versions, Israelite kings being often polygamists; but one of the wives takes precedence of the others, and occupies, like Bathsheba beside her son Solomon (1 Kings ii. 19), the post of honour at the king's right hand : in ' standeth,' or (R.V.) ' doth stand,' the poet is anticipating the future place of the newly-wedded princess.

And now the poet turns to the queen, first (*v.* 10 f.) addressing her, and then (*v.* 12) describing her. She is youthful, we may suppose, and inexperienced: so he offers her some words of fatherly advice and encouragement suited to the occasion; he counsels her to forget her old home, and surrender herself to her new lord.

10 ' Hearken, O daughter, and see, and incline thine ear ;
    forget also thine own people and thy father's house.

We are reminded here of the Homeric phrase, εἰς εὐνὴν φοιτῶντε, φίλους λήθοντε τοκῆας.

---

[1] Lit. *precious, valued ;* often of precious stones (2 Sam. xii. 30) ; of the 'sons of Zion,' once comparable to fine gold, but now esteemed only as ' earthen pitchers,' Lam. iv. 2. Cf. the cognate verb, *be precious,* of a life, 2 Kings i. 13, *al.*

XLV]   STUDYING THE PSALTER

> 11 And when the king desireth thy beauty
> (for he is thy lord), then bow thyself unto him—

viz. in homage (Gen. xxiii. 7 ; 1 Kings i. 23, etc.) : let her pay her husband—here called 'lord,' as Sarah calls Abraham 'lord' in Genesis xviii. 12—befitting respect and submission. 'God' in P.B.V., is a gloss, derived from the Vulgate, and expressing, in a Christian sense, the current Messianic interpretation of the Psalm. But in the 'Great Bible' of Coverdale (1539), from which the P.B.V. is taken, it is shown, like other additions of the same kind (e.g. in Ps. i. 5), to be no part of the Hebrew text, by being placed within parentheses and printed in smaller type than the body of the Psalm. In early P.B. Psalters, and in the 'Sealed Book' of 1662, these distinguishing marks are still preserved, but they have since been gradually dropped. Their omission, as Bishop Westcott observes, is 'very greatly to be regretted.' See further my *Parallel Psalter*, pp. xix.-xx.

Next the queen is further encouraged, upon entering her new home, with the thought of the deference and respect which she will

THE METHOD OF [PSALM

there receive, and of the eagerness with which gifts will be offered to her to win her favour.

V. 12 is difficult ; we must, it seems, adopt one of two interpretations. We may (1) suppose that a verb has fallen out, and render substantially as is done in A.V. and R.V.—

12 And the daughter of Tyre [shall come] with gifts,[1]
 the richest of the people shall intreat thy favour.

In this case the ' daughter of Tyre' will be the people of Tyre, personified, like the daughter of Zion, of Judah,' etc. ; and this wealthy commercial nation will be represented as coming to court the favour of the royal bride.

Or (2) we may keep the text as it stands, and render the opening words as a vocative—

12 And, O daughter of Tyre,[2] with gifts
 the richest of the people shall intreat thy favour.

---

[1] I.e. במנחה [תבוא]. The existing text cannot be rendered as is done in A.V., R.V. ; and the construction of בת צר with a *plural* verb is an objection to Ewald's rendering of the same text, adopted in the *Parallel Psalter*.

[2] For a vocative introduced by ' and,' without another vocative preceding, see Joel ii. 23. 'ובני ציון גילו וג ' And, O children of Zion, be glad,' etc.

Upon this interpretation, the 'daughter of Tyre' will be the royal bride herself, who will in this case be a Tyrian princess, or at least a princess of Tyrian extraction, like Athaliah.

There follows a description of the queen's splendid bridal attire and of the state procession, in which, accompanied by a long train of attendants, she is escorted from her own apartments to the royal palace—

13 All glorious[1] is the king's daughter within (her chamber) ;
her clothing is of chequer-work, inwrought with gold.

'Within'[2] means within a temple, palace, or, presumably, other building ; here, appar-

---

[1] Lit. (if the text is correct) *The whole of gloriousness*, a hyperbole. Cf. xxxix. 5, lit. *the whole of vanity*.

[2] The Hebrew is lit. *face-wards*, i.e. properly, in the inmost part of a hall or presence-chamber, where the throne would be facing those who enter it by the door at the further end (cf. the ἐνώπια παμφανόωντα of Homer), as of the Tent of Meeting (Lev. x. 18), the Temple (1 Kings vi. 18, 19 ; 2 Chron. xxix. 16), a palace (2 Kings vii. 11 ; 2 Chron. xxix. 18). The rendering 'within' (P.B.V., A.V.) suggests naturally 'inwardly,' 'within her own person' ; but this is quite alien to the usage of the Hebrew word.

ently (Kirkpatrick), within the residence in Jerusalem to which she had been brought, and where she now stands, decked in bridal attire, ready to be conducted in state to the king's palace (*vv.* 14, 15). To render with R.V. 'within (the palace)' anticipates unduly *vv.* 14, 15, where the queen is first brought to it. Some modern scholars, however, for פְּנִימָה מִמִּשְׁבְּצוֹת read בְּמִשְׁבְּצוֹת פְּנִינִם, i.e.

13 All glorious is the king's daughter;
    of *pearls in* filigree-settings of gold is her clothing.

For the rendering filigree-settings, see note [1] below.

'Chequer work' was some kind of decorative work, probably something of the nature of a 'check,'[1] whether, if of one colour, *quilted work*,[2] or, if of different colours, a *coloured check* : it was the material prescribed for the high priest's tunic (Exod. xxviii.

---

[1] In Exodus xxviii. 11, 13, 14, 20 the same word is used of the plaited gold settings of gems (A.V., R.V. 'ouches,' a now obsolete word for the frame in which a jewel is set : better, *filigree work*).

[2] See A. R. S. Kennedy's elaborate article, WEAVING, in the *Encycl. Bibl.* iv. 5288.

STUDYING THE PSALTER

4, 39) : here the fabric of the queen's dress is further decorated by being crossed, or varied in some way, with gold thread ; cf. Vergil's *picturatas auri subtemine vestes* (*Aen.* 3. 483).

14 In variegated raiment shall she be escorted unto the king ;
    the virgins her companions following her shall be brought unto thee.
15 With gladness and rejoicing shall they be escorted ;
    they shall enter into the king's palace.

V. 14. *Riḳmah* certainly means *variegated* fabric (see Ezek. xvii. 3, where it is used of the plumage of a bird), and probably fabric *embroidered* in colours (see Kennedy, *Enc. Bibl.* iv. 5289). The ' work of the variegator ' is prescribed for the screens of the Tent of Meeting and for the sash of the high priest (Exod. xxvi. 36, xxvii. 16, xxviii. 39) : see also Judges v. 30 ; Ezek. xvi. 10, 13, xxvii. 7, 16, 24, *al.*

V. 15. The king meets the procession escorting the bride ; and they enter the royal palace together. Cf. 1 Macc. ix. 37, 39 : ' The children of Jambri were making a great marriage, and were bringing the bride from Nadabath with a great train, a daughter of one of the great nobles of Canaan . . . And the bridegroom came forth, and his friends and his brethren, to meet them with timbrels and minstrels and many weapons.' And the poet closes (*v.* 16) with happy wishes and anticipations for the future, addressed to the royal bridegroom : of the offspring of his marriage he may make princes—as Rehoboam, we are told, stationed his sons in various cities of Judah (2 Chron. xi. 23)—who may represent him in different parts of his realm ; and (*v.* 17) his memory will be perpetuated with undying fame, not in Israel only, but among other nations as well—

16 Instead of thy fathers shall be thy children,
    whom thou shalt make princes in all the land.[1]
17 I will make mention of thy name in all generations :
    therefore shall the peoples give thanks unto thee
        for ever and ever.

The Psalm thus celebrates, in a high and

[1] Or, *in all the earth*—for many peoples (cf. *vv.* 6*c*, 17*b*) will have been embraced in his domain. The Hebrew is ambiguous, and may bear either meaning.

noble strain, the nuptials of an Israelite king. It is Messianic, in so far as it portrays an *ideal*. The king, whoever he was, whom the poet addresses is invested by him with ideal attributes : he is the impersonation of high virtues and perfections ; he is fairer than the children of men, graciousness is shed over his lips, therefore he is blessed of God for ever ; he is to carry on a crusade on behalf of the faithful, the humble, and the righteous ; he loves righteousness and hates wickedness, and therefore extraordinary blessings and happiness are showered upon him. The Psalm thus falls into line with other Psalms and prophecies, in which similar thoughts are expressed and similar ideals projected—the 2nd and the 72nd, for instance, and with the 110th. These Psalms express promises or hopes not fulfilled by any actual monarch of Israel ; they portray the king, not simply as what he was, but as what he should or might be ; in other words, they portray an *ideal*. They are thus, to use the technical expression, *typically* Messianic. And so, though sound exegesis will not permit $v.$ 7 to be quoted, as

METHOD OF STUDYING PSALTER

it was wont to be quoted, as a proof of the Divinity of Christ, the Psalm may still be read with perfect propriety in our Church on Christmas Day, as setting forth a great ideal of kingly virtues and kingly rule, which Christ realised in the transfigured and spiritualised realm of David in which He assumed the throne.

PSALM LXXII

PSALM LXXII

THE poet prays that God will confer upon the king the gifts that will enable him to fulfil the ideal of his office. Thus equipped, may he prove himself the righteous ruler who secures for his subjects justice and peace; and may he, as the reward of his upright rule, reign from sea to sea, receive the homage of distant nations, and look with satisfaction upon the prosperity of his people.

> 1 Give the king thy judgements, O God,
>   and thy righteousness unto the king's son.

The poet prays God to give the king a store of His 'judgements,' or decisions, that he may appropriate and apply them when cases come before him for judgment; and His 'righteousness,' that it may in the same way be expressed in the decisions that he gives.

In *vv.* 2–7 the consequences of the king's being thus equipped for his rule are developed:

may he judge the poor—those common victims of oppression and injustice under an Oriental government—righteously ; may his people also themselves live righteously, and enjoy the fruits of good government and peace !

> 2 May he judge thy people with righteousness,
>   and thy poor with judgement !
> 3 May the mountains bear peace to the people,
>   and the hills righteousness ! [1]
> 4 May he judge the poor of the people ;
>   may he save the children of the needy,
>   and crush the oppressor !

V. 2. With *righteousness* and *judgement,* as David did (2 Sam. viii. 15) ; and in accordance with the ideal, Jer. xxiii. 5.

Thy poor. Or *thine afflicted* (or, *humbled ones*), which is what the Hebrew word used properly means. So *vv.* 4, 12. See the article 'Poor' in Hastings' *Dict. of the Bible,* where the usage of the term is more fully explained.

In *v.* 3 the Hebrew has ' through righteousness.' But this greatly mars the parallelism of the verse, and doubtless Duhm is right in supposing that ' through righteousness ' is an

---

[1] Hebrew text, *through righteousness.* See the note.

LXXII] STUDYING THE PSALTER

error of transcription due to the fact that (in the Hebrew) the same expression (בצדקה) occurs in *v.* 2*a*. For the figure of ' bearing' (viz. as *fruit*) cf. Isaiah xlv. 8 (' salvation,' i.e. deliverance, and ' righteousness,' to spring out of the earth). Peace and righteousness (as a civic virtue, among the people), the effects of a righteous rule, are viewed poetically as a fruit or growth of the mountains and hills. For the ideal picture cf. Isaiah xxxii. 15-17 : ' Until the spirit be poured upon us from on high. . . . Then judgement shall dwell in the wilderness, and righteousness shall abide in the garden-land ; and the work of righteousness shall be peace, and the effect of righteousness quietness and confidence for ever.'

5 May he prolong (his days)[1] as long as the sun endureth,[2]
   and before the moon, through all generations !
6 May he come down like rain upon the mown grass,
   as showers, (even) drops [3] upon the earth !

---

[1] Hebrew text, *May they fear thee.* See the note.

[2] Heb. *with the sun.* See the same idiom in Daniel iv. 3 [Heb. iii. 23], lit. ' *with generation and generation.*'

[3] The word (*zarziph*) is peculiar, and occurs in the

THE METHOD OF [PSALM

7 In his days may righteousness[1] flourish ;
and abundance of peace till the moon be no more !

V. 5. May he prolong (his days). The Hebrew text has 'May they fear thee,'— words which might possibly be addressed to the king, though more probably, if they are correct, they are to be taken as addressed to God. In either case, however, and especially in the latter, the thought of the verse comes in abruptly, and is alien to the context. LXX read συμπαραμενεῖ, i.e. *shall continue*

Old Testament only here. It is cited as occurring once in the Talm. (*Yoma* 87a), of 'drops' scattered in throwing water from a bucket. Very possibly it is here a corruption of some verb meaning *to water* or *moisten*. יַזְרְפוּ, from זרף to *flow* (cited once from a late Midrash) does not give the right sense. If we might *infer* a verb, זרף, not otherwise known in Hebrew, either from Syr. זריפתא, *a heavy rain*, or Arab. *dharafa*, to *flow* (of tears), we could read יַזְרִיפוּ, 'that *make* the earth *to flow*.' Or we could read יַרְעִיפוּ, '*that make* the earth *to drop*' (cf. Ps. lxv. 12, R.V.m. [Heb. 13]). The best word, if the *ductus literarum* did not differ too widely from זרויף, would be יַרְוְיֻן, 'like showers that *water* the earth.' See Isaiah lv. 10 ; and for the form Psalm xxxvi. 8 [Heb. 9].

[1] Hebrew text, *the righteous*. See the note.

LXXII] STUDYING THE PSALTER

with, reading no doubt יאריך for יראוך ; and this yields a far better sense : ' May he *prolong* (his days) as long as the sun endureth ; ' the word, as Deuteronomy xvii. 20 and often ; for the ellipse of ' days,' see Ecclesiastes vii. 15. The hyperbolical wish as 1 Kings i. 31 ; Psalm xxi. 4, lxi. 6, 7 (above p. 83).

V. 6. May his rule be as gentle and beneficent as rain upon a mown meadow, or showers upon the earth. Cf. the similar comparison of the effects of a righteous rule in 2 Samuel xxiii. 3*c*, *d*, 4. The figure is carried on in the ' flourish' or ' blossom' of *v.* 7.

In *v.* 7 for *righteous*, LXX, Jerome, and the Syriac version have *righteousness*. The sense is not appreciably different : but the abstract term suits the parallel *peace* better, and the change in the Hebrew is only one of vocalisation.

Vv. 8-12. May his realm be wider than that of Solomon, may all enemies be subdued before him, may the most distant and famous peoples do him homage !

8 May he have dominion also from sea to sea,
    and from the River unto the ends of the earth !
9 May the desert-dwellers bow before him ;
    and his enemies lick the dust !
10 May the kings of Tarshish and of the isles render
    presents !
    may the kings of Sheba and Seba bring dues !
11 Yea, may all kings fall down to him !
    may all nations serve him !

V. 8. A poetical extension of the limits assigned by tradition to the empire of Solomon (1 Kings iv. 21 [Heb. v. 1]), 'And Solomon was ruling over all the kingdoms from the River unto the land of the Philistines, and as far as the border of Egypt' ; 24 'For he was having dominion [the same verb as here] over all the country beyond the River [i.e. west of it—viewed from the Babylonian standpoint], from Tiphsah [Thapsacus] as far as Gaza, over all the kings beyond the River.' 'The River,' as always in R.V. (e.g. Exod. xxiii. 31), when the word has a capital letter, is the Euphrates, *the* river κατ' ἐξοχὴν to the Hebrews. The greater part of *v*. 8 recurs *verbatim* in Zech. ix. 10*b*, in the description of the rule of the ideal king of the future,

STUDYING THE PSALTER

'And he shall speak peace unto the nations; and his rule shall be *from sea to sea, and from the River unto the ends of the earth.*'

V. 9. The 'desert-dwellers' are the wild Bedawin, the free sons of the desert, who will not readily own any superior. The rendering, though it fits the context excellently, is, however, uncertain, since elsewhere the word always means 'desert-*beasts*' (Ps. lxxiv. 14; Isa. xiii. 21 *al.*); hence several recent scholars would read *his adversaries* (צריו for ציים).

To *lick the dust* is a figure of abject submission: cf. the same words in Micah vii. 17; and to 'lick the dust of thy feet' in Isaiah xlix. 23. In Assyrian bas-reliefs captives are often represented as crouching down, with their faces on the ground, at their conqueror's feet.

V. 10. *Tarshish* is Tartessus in Spain (Gen. x. 4, Ezek. xxvii. 12 *al.*; and, as a distant country, as here, Isa. lxvi. 19). The *isles* or *coasts*—for the term used includes both—are in particular the isles and coasts of the Mediterranean Sea. The word is frequent in Deutero-Isaiah.

Shĕbā is the people known to the classical writers as *Sabœi*, Sabaeans. Their home was in the S.W. of Arabia, where numerous inscriptions, showing that they were a civilised and well-governed nation, have recently been discovered. They are several times mentioned in the Old Testament as a distant and wealthy people, famed for its gold, precious stones, and frankincense (1 Kings x. 1 ff., 10 ; Jer. vi. 20 ; Isa. lx. 6 ; Ezek. xxvii. 22). *Sĕbā* (also Gen. x. 7, a ' son' of Cush, and Isa. xliii. 3, xlv. 14, beside Egypt and Cush) was probably Σαβαί, a ' large city ' mentioned by Strabo on the west coast of the Red Sea, on the Adulitic Gulf.

The thought of *vv.* 10, 11 is no doubt suggested by 1 Kings iv. 21 [Heb. v. 1], ' they (viz. all kingdoms from the Euphrates to the border of Egypt) were bringing " presents "[1]

---

[1] The 'present' (Heb. *minḥah*) was not an ordinary gift, but an offering intended to conciliate the good-will of a superior,—often more or less expected, or compulsory, and a mark of subjection (cf. 2 Sam. viii. 2, 6) ; hence in Psalm lxxii. 10 'render' (implying a *due*) ; so 2 Kings xvii. 3 Heb. (where A.V. *marg.* had 'tribute,' as R.V. *marg.* has here).

LXXII] STUDYING THE PSALTER

and " served " Solomon ' ; x. 1, 10 (the Queen of Sheba and the gold, spices, and precious stones brought by her) ; x. 24 f. ('all the earth' were bringing him yearly ' presents ') ; x. 22 (the navy of ' Tarshish,'—though its voyages were, it is true, not to Tarshish but to Arabia).

Vv. 12-14. This far-reaching dominion and the worldwide homage which he will receive are the reward for his just and gracious rule. As before (*v.* 4), the king's special merit is his care for the poor and the oppressed.

12 For he will deliver the needy when he crieth,
    the poor also, and him that hath no helper.
13 He will have pity on the feeble and the needy,
    and the souls of the needy he will save.
14 He will redeem their soul from oppression and violence ;
    and precious will their blood be in his sight.

Their blood being ' precious,' he will take care that it is not unjustly shed.

Vv. 15-17. Three closing prayers, for the welfare of the king (*v.* 15), the fertility of the land and prosperity of the people (*v.* 16), and the honourable perpetuation of his name (*v.* 17).

THE METHOD OF [PSALM

15 And may he live, and may there be given unto him
   of the gold of Sheba !
   may prayer also be made for him continually !
   may he be blessed all the day !
16 May there be abundance[1] of corn in the land upon
   the top of the mountains !
   may the fruit thereof shake like Lebanon !
   and may men blossom out of the city like the herb
   of the earth !
17 May his name be for ever !
   before the sun may his name have increase :
   may all families of the earth [2] also bless themselves
   by him !
   may all nations call him happy !

In *v.* 15 ' may he live ' sounds like an echo of the regular exclamation, *May the king live!* (1 Kings i. 25 *al.*), which in Hebrew as in French (*Vive le roi !*) is the idiomatic equivalent of our *God save the king.* ' May the people not only greet him with the cus-

---

[1] So with a change of text. The Hebrew word found here is otherwise unknown, and the meanings that have been given to it are purely conjectural.

[2] So LXX ; see Genesis xii. 3. The words have probably accidentally fallen out in the Mass. text ; the verb ' bless themselves ' in the Hebrew lacks a subject and the addition improves the balance of lines 3 and 4 of *v.* 17.

LXXII] STUDYING THE PSALTER

tomary acclamation, and offer him the choicest gifts, but pray for his welfare and bless him, as the source of their happiness and prosperity ' (Kirkpatrick). In line 3 of the same verse, the P.B. Version *unto him* is not possible. There is no greater ambiguity in the sense of the Hebrew $b^{e'}ad$, than there is in that of the Greek ὑπέρ.

V. 16. The word פסת occurs nowhere else, and no satisfactory explanation of it has ever been given.[1] In the translation Lagarde's conjecture שפעת, *abundance* (of water, Job xxii. 11, xxxviii. 34 ; camels, Isa. lx. 6 ; horses, Ezek. xxvi. 10 ; men, 2 Kings ix. 9 twice) has been followed.

Blossom . . . like the herb of the earth. Their numbers and their freshness are the *tertium comparationis* : cf. Isaiah xxvii. 6 (' Israel shall *blossom* and bud '), Job v. 25*b* (' And thine offspring shall be *like the herb of the earth*'). May his people both flourish, and increase largely in numbers !

[1] *Handful* (A.V.) comes from a comparison of the Aram. *pas*, the *palm* of the hand (Dan. v. 5, 24) ; but this sense does not suit the context.

THE METHOD OF [PSALM

V. 17. *Have increase*, or *be propagated*, viz. by his descendants. The Hebrew word occurs only here, but *nīn*, ' progeny ' (Gen. xxi. 23 ; Job xviii. 19 ; Isa. xiv. 22 : A.V., R.V. *son*) would be cognate. The figure, as applied to a name, is, however, somewhat strange, and perhaps *be established* (יכן for ינן) should be read.

May all families of the earth also bless themselves by him ; i.e. use his name in blessing as a type of happiness, saying, ' God make me (or thee) like this king,' and so ' invoking for themselves the blessings which he enjoys, as the highest and best that they can imagine.' Jacob represents Israel as ' blessing themselves' by his two grandchildren, when he says (Gen. xlviii. 20), ' *By thee* shall Israel bless, saying, God make thee as Ephraim and as Manasseh.'[1] The same expression occurs in Genesis xxii. 18 and xxvi. 4 (which should be rendered, ' And *by* thy seed shall all

---

[1] Cf. the opposite custom of using a name in cursing (Jer. xxix. 22), ' Jehovah make thee like Zedekiah and like Ahab, whom the king of Babylon roasted in the fire.'

LXXII]   STUDYING THE PSALTER

nations of the earth *bless themselves*').[1]

The verses which follow form no part of the Psalm, but are the doxology closing the second Book of the Psalms, added by a compiler—

18 Blessed be the Lord God, the God of Israel,
   who only doeth wondrous things :
19 And blessed be his glorious name for ever :
   and let the whole earth be filled with his glory.
                Amen, and Amen.

Compare the similar doxologies closing the first, third and fourth Books (xli. 13 ; lxxxix. 52 ; cvi. 48).

The Psalm (notice *v.* 1), if it relates to an Israelite king, reads like a prayer on his accession ; what king, we do not know, but certainly one of the later ones—perhaps Josiah. This is shown both from the clear and easy style, which is just that of other Psalms which, upon independent grounds, are plainly not early ; and also from the allusions in *vv.* 10, 12-14 to the oppression of the poor and needy, which resemble strongly allusions of

[1] In Genesis xii. 3, xviii. 18, xxviii. 14 the form of the verb is different.

the same kind in Jeremiah and Ezekiel, and in Psalms of the same and later periods. The hopes and anticipations which the Psalm expresses for the king are suggested partly by reminiscences of Solomon's rule, partly by a sense of what the qualifications of a just ruler should be, in view of the social conditions of the time. The Psalm, if it was originally composed in view of an Israelite king, will be 'typically' Messianic in that it presents him under an *ideal* aspect, attributing to him an ideal rule of perfection and universality, extending to the ends of the earth, and attracting the homage of distant nations : the portrait in its entirety thus transcends that of an actual king, and depicts an *ideal* king, the father and protector of his people, the ruler worthy to command the homage of the world. It is, however, true that there are features in the Psalm that suggest a post-exilic date ; in particular the names in *v.* 10 read like reminiscences of such passages as Isa. xlii. 4, 10 ('isles'), xliii. 3, lx. 6, 9 ; and, as the Psalms are in their phraseology more usually dependent on the prophets than the prophets on the Psalms, there is a presumption that $v.$ 8 is more probably derived from Zechariah ix. 10 than Zechariah ix. 10 from $v.$ 8. Hence, as in this period there was no native king to whom $v.$ 1 could refer, and a reference to a foreign ruler —such as one of the Ptolemies—is not probable, it is possible, as even Kirkpatrick (p. 417) allows, that it ' does not refer to any particular king, but is a prayer for the establishment of the Messianic kingdom under a prince of David's line, according to prophecy,' a lyrical echo, in fact, of Zechariah ix. 10, and other passages of the prophets. Another possible view is that of Bäthgen, who remarks that $vv.$ 12-14 state more naturally the reason for $v.$ 7 than for $vv.$ 8-11 : accordingly he thinks that $vv.$ 1-7, 12-17 formed the original Psalm, referring to one of the later kings of Judah, and that $vv.$ 8-11 are an insertion made by a post-exilic poet for the purpose of imparting to the Psalm a Messianic character. Dr. Briggs' view is similar ; but he would include $v.$ 17c, d, with its reminiscences of Genesis xii. 3 and xxii. 18, in the post-exilic additions. Upon either of these views—upon the first **in**

METHOD OF STUDYING THE PSALTER

the intention of the original poet, upon the second as accommodated to the conception by a later poet—it will be directly Messianic. We cannot be sure which of these three views of the original application of the Psalm is correct ; but whichever be adopted, its general import will remain the same : as we have it, it is the portrait of an ideal ruler, either (1) foreshadowing, or (2 and 3) delineating directly, according to Jewish conceptions, the future ideal king, whom we call the ' Messiah.'

PSALM CX

PSALM CX

THE Psalm, as is evident from the terms used, is written of some Israelite king. Like the other Psalms of the same type—the 2nd or the 72nd, for instance—it depicts, under a particular aspect, the ideal glory of the theocratic king. It represents him as marching out with his people against his foes, as victorious, with Yahweh's help, against them, and, what is especially remarkable, as not king only, but priest.

> 1 'Tis Yahweh's oracle to my lord :
>   'Sit thou at my right hand,
>   until I make thine enemies thy footstool.'

(*'Tis*) *Yahweh's oracle* (*or whisper*) is the expression used so constantly by the prophets : in the English versions rendered, ' saith the LORD,' and so not distinguished from the ordinary Hebrew for ' saith the LORD.' The root of *n^e'ûm*, ' oracle,' means in Arabic to *utter a low sound* : hence the word in Hebrew probably denoted properly a *whispered utterance*, of a revelation heard quietly by the mental ear. The expression 'my lord' is one which recurs often in the books of Samuel and Kings (1 Sam. xxii. 12, 2 Sam. xiv. 20; more commonly followed by 'the king'); and it is the usual title by which the Israelite king is addressed by his courtiers. It is a prophet who here speaks; and he represents Jehovah as addressing the king, probably at his accession, with a solemn promise, conferring upon him the highest position of honour next himself ('on the right hand' as 1 Kings ii. 19; Ps. xlv. 9; Matt. x. 21), and assuring him of his protection until his foes are effectually subjugated. The 'footstool' is a truly Oriental figure: we see the conqueror with his feet on his vanquished foes, and we remember how Joshua (Josh. x. 24) bids his captains, after his defeat of the five kings, place their feet upon their necks (cf. 1 Kings v. 3 'Till Yahweh put them under the soles of Solomon's feet'). We have two pictorial illustrations of the passage, one, from Assyria, of a king planting his foot on the

cx] STUDYING THE PSALTER

necks of prostrate captives ; the other, from Egypt, of a king whose footstool is supported by nine heads of crouching captives, in two rows, one above the other, of five and four respectively. ' Until ' is naturally not exclusive of the period which follows : it is used to mark a turning-point with which a new epoch begins (cf. cxii. 8).

In what follows the poet expands this oracle, dwelling on the manner in which the promise will be fulfilled :—

2 Yahweh stretch out from Zion the sceptre of thy strength (saying),
  ' Rule thou in the midst of thine enemies.'

His palace on Zion is the centre of his dominion ; and thence will Yahweh Himself stretch out His sceptre, the symbol of His authority, bidding him rule unopposed, while his enemies are submissive and passive about him.

The poet next describes his success, in an ideal battle scene. He pictures him advancing to the combat, surrounded by his warriors, all equipped, and eager for the fray. We must discard here the now familiar rendering of the P.B. Version ('offer thee free-will offerings with an holy worship'); for it yields a completely false sense.

3 Thy people offer themselves willingly in the day of
   thy host:
   in holy adornments,[1] from the womb of the dawn,
   thine is the dew of thy young men.

Professor Cheyne's beautiful paraphrase may be quoted: 'Martial Israelites stream to the royal banner (comp. Jud. v. 2, 9, where the Hebrew for 'offer themselves freely' is cognate). It is an early morning muster; and suddenly (cf. 2 Sam. xvii. 11, 12) as the

> dewdrops which the sun
> Impearls on every leaf and every flow'r

(Milton's figure for the angel-hosts), and not less past counting than these, there seems to start up on all sides a youthful army, brimming over with that freshness and vigour of which " dew " in the prophets (Hos. xiv. 5, Isa. xxvi. 19) is the symbol.' In the expression 'from the womb of the morning,' the morning is poetically thought of as the mother of the

[1] Or, as Symm., Jer., with a very slight change (הררי for הדרי), *upon the holy mountains*.

cx]　STUDYING THE PSALTER

dew. The 'holy adornments,' if correct, allude probably to the warriors' gleaming weapons, called 'holy' because used in the service of Yahweh (comp. the common Hebrew expression, to 'consecrate' a war, or warriors, Joel iii. 9 ; Jer. xxii. 7 *al.*). But the plural (in the Hebrew) is strange : and very probably, with the smallest possible change in the Hebrew text (הררי for הדרי), we should read with Symmachus and Jerome ' on the holy *mountains* ' (viz. of Palestine).

An unexpected trait is next introduced :—

> 4 Jehovah hath sworn, and will not repent ;
>   'Thou art a priest for ever
>   after the manner of Melchizedek.'

The ruler addressed is not to be only king : he is to be solemnly inaugurated as priest, after the manner—the word does not mean ' order,' as we speak of an ' order ' of priesthood[1]

---

[1] דברה—a rare word, properly a *statement*, and so *plea*, *case* (Job v. 8),—acquires also meanings similar to those of דבר, properly *word*, then *thing, reason, case,* etc. So, as על דבר means often ' on *account* of ' (cf. ' for the *sake* of,' where ' sake ' is the German *Sache, thing, matter, case,* etc.), על דברת means ' on *account* of,' Eccles. iii. 18, viii. 2, and ' for the *reason* that,' vii. 14 ;

THE METHOD OF [PSALM

—after the manner, not of the Levitical or Aaronic priests, familiar at the time, but of *Melchizedek*, who, in the old primitive fashion, combined the offices of king and priest in his own person. Melchizedek, it seems, is referred to as a type of priest-king, consecrated by old tradition (Gen. xiv.), to which the ideal Israelite king, ruling at the same spot, must conform : Melchizedek united the two offices, and the ideal king must do the same. The name, suggesting ' King of righteousness,' might also be taken as prefiguring the character which the ideal king would bear. ' For ever,' we must remember, need not mean more than for the king's lifetime ; comp. ' a slave for ever ' (Deut. xv. 17 ; Job xl. 28), or ' shall serve him for ever ' (Exod. xxi. 6).

Vv. 5-7 continue the strain begun in *vv.* 2-3, and describe the victory which the **poet** pictures the king as gaining over his foes.

5 The Lord upon thy right hand
    shattereth kings in the day of his anger.

---

and as דבר means *case, reason, manner* (Deut. xv. 2, xix. 4 ; Jos. v. 4 ; 1 Kings ix. 15, xi. 27 ; Esth. i. 13), so דברה here has the force of *manner*.

6 He judgeth among the nations ;
    he filleth (the places) with dead bodies ;
    he shattereth the heads in pieces over a wide country.

Jehovah, standing at the king's right hand in his chariot, to assist and support him, will shatter kings in the day of His anger—His 'anger' against His foes (ii. 5, 12, xxi. 9), or heathen nations, often announced by the prophets : he will 'judge among the nations, fill (the places) with dead bodies, and shatter the heads in pieces over a wide country'; we see the enemy in flight, like the Canaanites before Barak, and the plains, far and near, are covered with the heads and corpses of the slain. The Psalm closes with a scene from the pursuit—

7 He drinketh of the wādy[1] by the way :
    therefore doth he lift up the head.

The king, exhausted in his course, like Jona-

[1] Heb. *naḥal*, corresponding to the Arabic *wādy*, often met with in books of travel in Palestine. We have no suitable English equivalent : 'brook' expresses too little ; 'torrent' too much ; 'stream' is too colourless ; 'river' is incorrect.

than, when he tasted the honey (1 Sam. xiv. 27, where ' his eyes were enlightened ' means that they brightened after faintness, i.e. he revived), is seen refreshing himself at a wādy flowing by ; revived and invigorated by the draught, with head erect, he will continue the pursuit till his triumph is complete.

The Psalm thus depicts a king, assured of the high favour and support of Yahweh, going forth to battle, surrounded by his warriors, and scattering his foes. The picture, it is plain, is an *ideal* one, based upon the experiences of the Israelite kings. We are reminded of David in his conflicts with Syrians or Edomites, Jehoshaphat victorious against the Moabites, or Uzziah subduing Philistines and Arabians. The date of the Psalm it is hardly possible to fix, except within relatively broad limits. But it will scarcely be an early one : it presupposes a time when the position and character of the king had been long reflected on, and had given occasion to ideal delineations. The word rendered *manner* occurs besides only in Job (v. 8) and the very late book, Ecclesiastes (iii. 18, vii. 14, viii. 2).

cx] STUDYING THE PSALTER

The position of the Psalm in the Psalter, also, does not suggest an early date. It is in the Fifth Book, and it is preceded and followed by Psalms certainly not earlier than the exile, and to all appearance later: cvii., cviii. (a composite Psalm), cix., cxi. ff. If pre-exilic, it will have been spoken of one of the later kings.

Several recent commentators [1] have thought one of the Maccabaean princes to be referred to. Jonathan, brother of Judas, who was chosen 'prince and leader' of the patriotic party after Judas' death in 161 B.C. (1 Macc. ix. 30 f.), was made by Alexander Balas, son of Antiochus Epiphanes, the 'King's Friend,' appointed by him high priest, and authorised to wear a purple robe and a crown of gold, the insignia of royalty (1 Macc. x. 18-20); he assumed the high-priestly vestments at the Feast of Booths, B.C. 153 (*ib. v.* 21). And Simon, Jonathan's brother, after Jonathan's

[1] See Cheyne, *Origin of the Psalter* (1891), pp. 22-29; and cf. Edghill, *Evidential Value of Prophecy*, p. 350 f.; Burney, *Interpreter*, Oct. 1909, p. 60; T. Witton Davies in the *Century Bible*, on Ps. cx., p. 223.

death (B.C. 143), was made by a decree of the people 'leader and high priest for ever, till there should arise a faithful prophet' (1 Macc. xiv. 41; cf. xiii. 42), capable of deciding doubtful points, like Elijah; he was also to be 'captain,' with supreme charge of all affairs of state (1 Macc. xiv. 42), and was authorised to wear purple and a buckle of gold (*ib. v.* 43). During his seven years' rule (B.C. 143-136) Simon gained many successes, restored the defences of his country, freed it from the yoke of the Syrian (1 Macc. xiii. 41, xiv. 26), and in particular, in 142, drove out of the Akra at Jerusalem the Syrian garrison which had occupied it for twenty-six years (1 Macc. xiii. 51; see i. 33 f.), and entered it 'with praise and palm-branches, and with harps, and cymbals, and viols, and with hymns and songs.' Simon's rule of peace and prosperity is depicted by the author of 1 Maccabees in Messianic colours (1 Macc. xiv. 4-15): the people 'tilled their land in peace, and the land gave her increase, and the trees of the plains their fruit: the old men sat in the streets, they talked all of them

CX]   STUDYING THE PSALTER

together of the good things, and the young men put on glorious and warlike apparel. . . . They sat each man under his vine and his fig-tree, and there was none to make them afraid. . . . And he strengthened all those of his people that were brought low : the low he searched out, and every lawless and wicked person he took away.' The poet of Psalm cx. might well have interpreted the decree of the people making Simon highpriest as embodying the purpose of Jehovah ; and Simon's many military successes might well have suggested to him the picture of a victorious campaign.

As Bäthgen says, the view is attractive : but it is not free from objection. In the Psalm one who is already a king is promised a priesthood ; but the Maccabees were themselves (1 Macc. ii. 1) of priestly descent, of the family of Joarib (1 Chron. xxiv. 7), though not of the high-priestly line ; Jonathan and Simon only became princes or kings on account of the prestige gained by their victories. They would thus have usurped the place of the legitimate high-priest. One wonders whether, in these circumstances, either Jonathan or Simon would have been addressed by a poet-prophet quite in the terms here used. It is also an objection to the same view that the Psalmist, to judge from the words, ' 'Tis Yahweh's whisper' (see above), speaks as a *prophet*, whereas in 1 Macc. the absence of a prophet is more than once deplored.[1] It is Bäthgen's view that the Psalm is a late one, and apparently that it is a Maccabaean one; but he supposes it to relate not to an actual king, but to the Messiah as he was pictured by the later Jews on the basis of the representations of the earlier prophets. The use of ' my lord,' which seems to suggest an actual king rather than one only pictured as present by the imagination, is some objection to this view, but not perhaps a fatal one; we may remember how vividly the author of Zechariah ix. 9 (probably *c.* 300 B.C.) pictures the Messianic king victoriously entering his capital. How the Jews thought of the Messiah in the late post-exilic age may be seen from an extract from Ps. xvii. of the so-called ' Psalms

[1] iv. 46 and ix. 27, as well as xiv. 41.

of Solomon,'[1] written probably shortly after Pompey's capture of Jerusalem in B.C. 70—

23 Behold, O Lord, and raise up unto them their king,
    the son of David, in the time which *thou* knowest, O God,
    that he may reign over Israel, thy servant.
24 And gird him with strength,
    that he may break in pieces unjust rulers.
25 Cleanse Jerusalem from the heathen that trample her down to destroy her,
    with wisdom, (and) with righteousness;
26 To thrust out sinners from the inheritance,
    to utterly destroy the haughtiness of sinners,
    and as a potter's vessels with a sceptre of iron
    to break in pieces all their substance;
27 To destroy ungodly nations with the word of his mouth,
    that at his rebuke nations may flee before him,
    and to convict sinners for the word of their heart.
28 And he shall gather together a holy people, whom he shall lead in righteousness,
    and he shall judge the tribes of the people that hath been sanctified by the Lord his God.
29 And he shall not suffer injustice to lodge in their midst;
    and none that knoweth wickedness shall dwell with them.

The poetry is obviously inferior to that of

[1] See Ryle and James, *Psalms of the Pharisees, commonly called the Psalms of Solomon*, 1891, p. 137 ff.

the Book of Psalms, and the entire description (which is continued to v. 51, and resumed in xviii. 6-10) is formed largely of phrases adapted from Psalm lxxii. and other passages of the Old Testament ; [1] but the representation of the Messiah as a conqueror dispersing his foes is common to both this ' Psalm of Solomon' and our Psalm ii. and cx. In the interpretation of Psalm cx., however, it does not make any real difference whether it portrays an actual king delineated with ideal features, or an ideal king delineated on the model of the actual king. But if the latter view be correct, and the Psalm refers primarily to the Messianic king, it cannot be an early one ; for it presupposes the development of the figure of the Messiah effected on the basis of the representations of the prophets.

In either case, however, the Psalm resembles in principle the Psalms which we have already considered. It depicts a king, transcending the historical reality, invested with an ideal dignity, and ideal powers. The king depicted receives a twofold solemn pro-

[1] See for particulars Ryle and James, pp. lii.-lviii.

CX] STUDYING THE PSALTER

mise, of an exalted and secure position beside Yahweh, ensuring him success against his foes, and of a perpetual priesthood. David and Solomon, and perhaps other kings, though not regular priests, exercised priestly functions in offering sacrifice and blessing the people (2 Sam. vi. 17; 1 Kings iii. 5, viii. 14); Melchizedek, the ancient king of Salem, was said to have been both king and priest: and the same privilege is here solemnly bestowed on the ideal king. Jeremiah (xxx. 21) also speaks of the future ideal ruler as enjoying the right of priestly access to God: 'and its [the people's] noble shall be from itself, and its ruler shall proceed from its midst [i.e. their ruler will be a native prince, not a foreigner]; and I will cause him to draw near, and he shall approach unto me [i.e. he will have the right of access to the altar, and enjoy priestly privileges; comp. the same two words in Num. xvi. 5; Lev. xxi. 21, 23; Ezek. xliv. 13], saith Yahweh.'

Our Lord, however, speaks of the Psalm as written by David (Matt. xxii. 43=Mark xii. 36=Luke xx. 42). We must, however, remember that our Lord was not pronouncing a judgement on a point of literary criticism, but arguing against the Pharisees. The question of the authorship of the Psalm was not one with which He was dealing. Nor can we expect our Lord to pronounce judgement upon matters which lay outside the scope of His Ministry, and opened questions which His hearers would not comprehend, or be ready to consider. Our Lord takes His opponents upon their own ground, and does not complicate the question by raising an issue irrelevant to His main contention. The real issue was not, Who wrote the Psalm ? but, What does the Psalm say ? The figure depicted by the Psalmist is invested by him with such august attributes that the Jews recognised in it the Messiah : must they not, therefore, look for a Messiah who was more than a mere human descendant of David, especially at a time when David's family was stripped of its dignity and reduced to insignificance ? and ought they, therefore, to stumble at His claims ? [1]

---

[1] See further on this subject Kirkpatrick's note in

In the Israelite monarchy was foreshadowed the sovereignty to be exercised in the future by David's son. Elevated, extended, and spiritualised, the aims and objects of the monarchy of David are the aims and objects of the Kingdom of Christ. Like other prophecies, the prophecy of this Psalm starts from the present and looks out into the future. We see an earthly monarch, engaging in a struggle of flesh and blood, and fighting bloody battles with his enemies : ' He filleth (the places) with dead bodies ; he shattereth the heads in pieces over a wide country.' Here is the starting-point in the Psalmist's own present. We see again traits which pass beyond the literal reality, and lend themselves to an ideal picture : ' Sit thou on my right hand until I make thine enemies thy footstool ' ; ' Thou art a priest for ever after the manner of Melchizedek.' It is in virtue of such traits as these that the Psalm is Messianic, prefiguring one in whom they are truly realised. The language of *v.* 1*a* became in early Christian thought the natural

the *Cambridge Bible*, p. 662 f. ; Edghill, *Evidential Value of Prophecy*, pp. 421 ff., 498 f.

expression for the exaltation of our Lord after His Ascension ; it is so applied on several occasions by the Apostles,[1] it was incorporated at an early date in the Christian Creed, where it is familiar to us still. Not, indeed, that in reciting the words, ' And sitteth on the right hand of God the Father Almighty,' we mean to affirm that either the right hand or the left can be predicated of a spiritual Being ; but we adopt the language originally applied to the ideal Israelite king as an apt *symbolical* expression for the unique dignity reserved for his Divine Son.[2] And in the Epistle to the Hebrews it is shown how the promise of a priesthood, superior to that of Aaron, solemnly inaugurated, and unchangeably constituted, pointed to the abrogation of the Levitical priesthood, and received its fulfilment in the person and office of Christ.

---

[1] Eph. i. 20 ; Col. iii. 1 ; Heb. i. 3, viii. 1, x. 12, xii. 2 ; 1 Pet. iii. 22 ; Rev. iii. 21. Cf. also the use of the phraseology of Ps. cx. 1*b* ('Until I make,' etc.), in 1 Cor. xv. 25, Heb. x. 13 ; and the quotations of the entire verse in Acts ii. 34, 35, Heb. i. 13.

[2] Cf. Edghill, p. 556 f.

PSALM XL

PSALM XL

THIS Psalm consists of two parts, differing widely in character and tone. The first part (*vv.* 1-12) is marked by vigour and originality of expression ; the second part (*vv.* 13-17) is constructed largely of conventional phrases ; it occurs also, with slight textual variations, as a separate Psalm (Ps. lxx.). In the first part, the predominant thoughts are those of gratitude for deliverance, and of spiritual service ; in the second part the Psalmist is beset by foes, and prays earnestly for speedy deliverance.

The occasion of the Psalm we do not know : but the case is one in which the contents of the Psalm speak so plainly that, if we did know it, we should hardly understand the Psalm better. It is certainly much later than the age of David.

The Psalmist begins by describing the

danger he had been in, and how, after patient waiting upon God, he had been rescued from it—

1 I waited waitingly for Jehovah ;
   and he inclined unto me, and heard my cry.
2 And he brought me up out of the roaring pit,[1] out of the miry clay ;
   and set my feet upon a crag, making firm my goings.

In *v.* 2 he compares himself to a person sinking in a watery pit, or floundering in a morass, where his feet had no support (cf. Ps. lxix. 2, 14 f.) ; but he had been rescued

[1] 'Horrible' (P.B.V., A.V., R.V.) is a paraphrase ; שאון cannot by any possibility *mean* 'horrible.' Elsewhere שאון is a stronger synonym of המון, and means a *din*, or what we call a *roar*—of the waves or a great host of men (Isa. xvii. 12*b*, 13 [R.V. *rushing*], xiii. 4 [R.V. *tumult*], Ps. lxv. 7 [R.V. *roaring*]), or the *uproar* [R.V.m. *tumult*] of a gay city (Isa. v. 14) ; or the *din* or *crash* of battle (Am. ii. 2 ; Hos. x. 14 [A.V., R.V. *tumult*] ; Jer. xxv. 31). Hence the only sense, consistent with usage, that the word can have here is *roaring*. The expression is obviously figurative ; and the Psalmist may have thought of a huge pit or subterranean dungeon (the word *bôr* denotes both), at the bottom of which were roaring waters. 'Destruction' (R.V.m. *alt.*) is also a meaning which שאון nowhere else has. See further *Oxf. Heb. Lex.*, p. 980 f.

from this perilous position, and placed securely on a rock. The figures, as often in the Psalms, are derived from the country scenery of Palestine. What the danger was we do not know: it may have been sickness, or persecution, or some other bodily peril ; or, if the speaker be the nation, it may have been the Babylonian exile : cf. Lam. iii. 53-56, where the nation, after the capture of Jerusalem by the Chaldaeans, is described figuratively as a prisoner in a ' pit ' or dungeon— the same word as here—with its mouth closed by a stone, and with the water flowing over his head.

> 3 And he put a new song in my mouth,
>   even praise unto our God :
>   many will see, and fear,
>   and will trust in Jehovah.

The occasion was one adapted to evoke the Psalmist's gratitude, and worthy to be celebrated by a ' new ' song, worthy of the new occasion (comp. the same expression Ps. xxxiii. 3, xcvi. 1, and xcviii. 1 [from Isa. xlii. 10], cxliv. 9, cxlix. 1) : the contemplation of God's mercy and power, shown in his de-

THE METHOD OF [PSALM

liverance, will arouse in others feelings of reverence and trust.

4-5. Happy those who trust in a God, whose goodness to His people is unspeakable !

4 Happy is the man that hath made Jehovah his trust,
    and hath not turned to[1] the proud boasters, or such
      as turn aside to lies.[2]
5 Many things hast *thou* done, O Jehovah, my God,
    even thy wondrous works and thy thoughts towards
      us ;
    there is none to be compared unto thee ;
    if I would declare and speak (of them),
    they are more than can be told.

4*b*. By the 'proud boasters'[3] are meant loud, self-confident, and worldly men, who

[1] Or, *looked at, regarded.*
[2] Or, *and them that have lyingly fallen away* (Cheyne), Hupfeld, Bäthgen, *al.*
[3] The word used occurs only here : but the root and other derivatives occur in the sense of *boastful pride* : Isaiah iii. 5 A.V., R.V., ' behave himself proudly ' ; Psalm xc. 10 R.V., ' Yet is their *pride* but labour and sorrow ' (the ἀλαζονία τοῦ βίου of 1 John ii. 16) ; and in ' Rahab,' the name of the proud sea-monster in Job ix. 13, xxvi. 12, and of boastful Egypt in Isaiah xxx. 7 (cf. R.V.m.) and elsewhere. מרחבה. ' pride ' or ' raging ' (of a tyrannical oppressor), must also be read

XL] STUDYING THE PSALTER

by their ostentatious self-assertion encourage others to rely upon them, and imitate their bad example. Happy the man who is content with God's help, and does not court their patronage or friendship ! Those who—not (P.B.V.) ' go about with lies,' but—*turn aside to lies* (A.V., R.V.) are those who desert God for false objects of reliance, vain aims and hopes, empty ambitions, or even, it may be, for false gods (cf. the same word in Amos ii. 4). The other possible rendering, *them that have lyingly fallen away* [1] (i.e. *false apostates*), would denote apostasy distinctly.

6. Jehovah, on the contrary, is a sure ground of trust : He is the author of unnumbered benefits to Israel.

7-9. What adequate response can the Psalmist make for such goodness ? And so he enumerates, like Amos (v. 21-24), Hosea (vi. 6), Isaiah (i. 11-17), Jeremiah (vii. 21 ff.),

---

for מדהבה (which cannot mean either ' golden city ' or ' exactress ') in Isaiah xiv. 4 ; notice the same parallel ' oppress ' (like a task-master) in Isaiah iii. 5.

[1] For the syntax in this case, cf. Psalm lix. 5 [Heb. 6] ; and see G.-K. § 128*x*.

Micah (vi. 8), and other prophets, the great spiritual truth that the true response to God's works of love consists not in material sacrifices, or even in servile submission to an unloved superior, but in the devotion of the heart, in obedience to God's will, as something in which man delights, and which has its home in his inmost being.

6 Sacrifice and meal-offering thou hast no delight in ;
    ears hast thou digged for me ;
    burnt-offering and sin-offering thou hast not asked :
7 Then said I, ' Lo, I am come ;
    ' in the roll of the book it is prescribed to me :
8 ' I delight to do thy pleasure, O my God ;
    ' and thy law is in my inmost parts.'

6. *Ears hast thou digged for me.* The expression, if the text is correct, must mean, Thou hast endowed me with the faculty of hearing and obeying, ' digged ' being an allusion to the shape of the ears, channels scooped out, as it were, and conveying words to the mind.[1]

---

[1] It lies near to say, ' to the *brain* ' ; but in the psychology of the Hebrews the heart, not the head, is the seat of intelligence. See e.g. Hosea vii. 11 ' Ephraim

7. ' I am come ' is a synonym of the usual
' Here I am ' (Heb. ' Behold me ! '). Like
a servant responding to his master's summons,
the Psalmist replies, ' Here I am, ready to
fulfil thy behests : in the roll of the book
it is '—not ' written of me,' a most misleading
rendering, but—' written, or prescribed, *to
me* ' (see the same Hebrew with this meaning
in 2 Kings xxii. 13). The reference may be
in particular to Deuteronomy, in which,
though ceremonial duties are not repudiated,
a spiritual service, consisting of loyal devotion
to God, and deeds of charity, mercy and
benevolence towards men is strongly and
repeatedly insisted on.

8. A climax on *v.* 7. The Psalmist not
only *knows* what God demands, but has a
delight in doing it. The thought of the

is a silly dove, *without heart* ' [we should say, colloquially,
' without a *head* '] ; Jeremiah v. 21 ' O foolish people,
without *heart* ' (A.V., R.V. ' without understanding ') ;
and frequently. There is no indication that the Hebrews
were aware of the real functions of the brain. They
regarded the heart as the region of intelligence, and
the ' soul,' kidneys (' reins '), and bowels (cf. on *v.* 8),
as the seats of different emotions.

verse corresponds to what is so often inculcated in Deuteronomy, to love, or serve, God 'with *all* the heart and *all* the soul,' i.e. with the intellect and the emotions alike (Deut. iv. 29, vi. 5, x. 12, xi. 13, xiii. 3, xxvi. 16, xxx. 2, 6, 10). 'In my inmost parts' is here lit. 'in my bowels.' The bowels, in Hebrew psychology, are the seat of deep emotion (Job xxx. 27 ; Jer. iv. 19 ; Lam. i. 20, ii. 11), or warm affection (Isa. xvi. 11, lxiii. 15 ; Jer. xxxi. 20 ; Cant. v. 4) : so the law, the Psalmist means to say, lay deep in his affections.

In Hebrews x. 5-7, *vv.* 6-8*a* are quoted, with a remarkable variation, adopted from the LXX, *a body hast thou prepared for me*, for the purpose of contrasting the perfect obedience of Christ with the inefficacy of the sacrifices of the Law. The origin of the variant is uncertain : it *may* rest upon a various reading in the Hebrew ; though naturally, if this is the case, it can have no claim to represent the original text, the sense expressed by it being too incongruous with the context. It is, however, a plausible sug-

XL]   STUDYING THE PSALTER

gestion that it originated partly in a corruption in the Greek (for which there are many parallels in the LXX), partly either in a different reading in the Hebrew, or in a misrendering of the existing text : 'body' having come in for 'ears' through the corruption of ΗΘΕΛΗCΑCΩΤΙΑ into ΗΘΕΛΗCΑCCΩΜΑ, and κατηρτίσω either being an ungrammatical rendering of כנת (i.e. כָּנְתָ)[2] for כרת, or representing (correctly) a reading הכנת (i.e. הֲכִנְתָ). The author of the Epistle to the Hebrews shows no immediate knowledge of the Hebrew text of the Old Testament, and treats the LXX as authoritative.[3] He quoted, therefore, the passage as he found it, the word 'body' at

[1] Cf. F. W. Mozley, *The Psalter of the Church* (the LXX of the Psalms compared with the Heb., with explanatory notes), 1905, pp. xv., 73 (where instances of similar corruptions are quoted).

[2] The Qal of כון, though found in Phoen., Arab., Eth. (in which languages it has the weakened sense of *to be*), is not in use in Heb. ; and if it were in use, would be an intransitive verb, and could not therefore signify 'establish' or 'prepare.'

[3] Westcott, *Ep. to the Hebrews*, p. 479.

once suggesting its applicability to Christ. In so far, however, as the rendering of the LXX can be brought into harmony with the context—which is often quite impossible with the renderings of the LXX—the ' body ' must be regarded as the organ of obedience : ' as the ear is the instrument for receiving the divine command, so the body is the instrument for fulfilling it ' (Kirkpatrick). On the sense in which the passage is quoted in the epistle with reference to Christ, see below.

Vv. 9-11. The Psalmist declares that he has given open expression to his gratitude by proclaiming publicly God's goodness towards him ; and that he anticipates the continuance of His favour.

9 [1]I have proclaimed glad tidings of[1] righteousness in
a great congregation :
lo, I will not restrain my lips,
Jehovah, *thou* knowest.
10 I have not hid thy righteousness within my heart ;
I have declared thy faithfulness and thy salvation :
I have not concealed thy kindness and thy truth
from the great congregation.

---

[1] In the Hebrew the word (בשרתי)=$ε\dot{υ}ηγγελισάμην$, as the LXX rightly render it.

11 Thou, Jehovah, wilt not restrain thy compassion
from me ;
let thy kindness and thy truth continually preserve
me.

Righteousness is that attribute of God in
virtue of which He acts justly,[1] and gives
men—here, in particular, the Psalmist—their
due ; *faithfulness* expresses His consistency
with His revealed character ; *salvation*[2] is

[1] Cf. Isaiah xli. 2, of Jehovah's guiding Cyrus in his
career of conquest ; 10, of His protecting Israel, and
restoring it to Palestine ; xlii. 6, of His call of ideal
Israel, 21 ; xlv. 13 of His prospering Cyrus that he may
release the Jewish exiles.

[2] The Heb. words for 'salvation' (יְשׁוּעָה, יֵשַׁע
and, as here, תְּשׁוּעָה—the last formed by a false analogy,
as if from יָשַׁע) mean properly, as Arabic shows, *breadth*,
spaciousness (cf. the participle of the cognate verb in
Matt. vii. 13, in an Arabic version of the Gospels, for
πλατεῖα) ; they thus in Hebrew denote primarily a
material deliverance, as appears very clearly from 1
Samuel xi. 9, 13, xix. 5 (so the syn. ישועה, Ex. xiv. 13, 1
Sam. xiv. 45 *al.*). In the Psalms the context shows that
all these words usually mean similarly either *deliverance*
or *welfare* (Job xxx. 15, A.V., R.V.), *well-being*, as iii. 2
(A.V., R.V. *help* ; so lx. 11), 8 (R.V.m. *victory* : so xx. 5,
xliv. 4, cxix. 4), xiii. 5, xviii. 2, 35, 50, xxxiii. 17 (' safety '),
xlii. 5 (A.V. *help*, R.V. *health*, i.e. *welfare* [' Heil '] ;

the fulness of deliverance and consequent well-being, resulting from the exercise of these attributes; *kindness and truth*—often linked together, whether denoting human (Gen. xxiv. 49; 2 Sam. ii. 6 *al.*) or divine (Exod. xxxiv. 6; Ps. lvii. 3, lxi. 7) qualities —express the combined warmth and trustworthiness of the Divine heart. These Divine attributes have been the Psalmist's themes, in his public recital[1] of God's mercies; they have been manifested in the deliverance of His servant—and it may be, of others, his compatriots or co-religionists, at the same time; and he prays hopefully for their continuance. For now fresh troubles encompass

see my *Parallel Psalter*, p. 473), xlii. 11 and xliii. 5 (also *health*), lxxiv. 12, cxxxii. 16 (P.B.V. *health*, as li. 14 and elsewhere; see above), etc.; and in the present passage. In the prophets, especially Deutero-Isaiah, it is often used in a larger sense of a *material deliverance accompanied by spiritual blessings* (e.g. Isa. xlix. 6); and this leads on to the purely spiritual sense which σωτηρία, its equivalent in the LXX, acquires in the New Testament.

[1] 'A great congregation,' as xxii. 25, xxxv. 18: cf. xxii. 22; and 'congregations' in Psalm xxvi. 12, lxviii. 26.

XL]   STUDYING THE PSALTER

him, and the Psalm closes with an earnest prayer for speedy deliverance—

12 For innumerable evils have encompassed me,
  mine iniquities have overtaken me,[1] and I cannot see ;[2]
  they are more in number than the hairs of mine head, and my heart hath failed[3] me.
13 Be pleased, Jehovah, to deliver me ;
  Jehovah, haste thee to help me.
14 Let them be ashamed and abashed together, that seek my soul to sweep it away ;[4]
  let them turn backward and be brought to confusion, that delight in my hurt.
15 Let them be appalled by reason of their shame[5]
  that say unto me, Aha, aha.
16 Let all those that seek thee rejoice and be glad in thee ;
  let such as love thy salvation say continually, ' Jehovah be magnified.'

---

[1] Viz. in their consequences, ' like an avenging Nemesis ' (Hupf.) ; cf. for the word Deut. xxviii. 2, 15.

[2] Sight fails him, he cannot see which way to turn, through the distress and anxiety caused by his troubles ('evils'). Compare xxxviii. 10.

[3] Heb. *forsaken*. Heart = courage ; cf. xxvii. 14, xxxi. 24, lxxvi. 5.

[4] Cf., in the Heb., Genesis xviii. 23, 24 ; Numbers xvi. 26 ; 1 Samuel xxvi. 10 ('destroy' and 'consume' obliterate the distinctive figure of the original).

[5] I.e. the disgrace that will fall upon them.

17 But I am poor and needy ;
   the Lord thinketh of me :
   thou art my help and my deliverer ;
   O my God, make no tarrying.

As has been already remarked, it is strange that a Psalm so original in thought and expression as *vv.* 1-12 should end in such conventional phrases as form the bulk of *vv.* 13-17[1] (which, as was said before, recurs, with insignificant differences, as Ps. lxx.) ; and it is difficult to think that both parts of the Psalm are by the same poet. On the other hand, *v.* 12 is not a natural ending to the Psalm, and seems to require a prayer to follow it. It may be that the original poet, for some reason or other, adopted *vv.* 13-17 as his conclusion ; it may be that the original ending was lost, and a compiler attached *vv.* 13-17 to the part of the original Psalm which remained. On such matters we can but speculate. If, however, *vv.* 1-12 belong to-

---

[1] *V.* 13*b*, as xxii. 19 *end*, xxxviii. 22*a* ; *v.* 14 closely resembling xxxv. 4, with a phrase substituted from xxxv. 26*a* ; *v.* 15 *end*, as xxxv. 21 ; *v.* 16 very similar to xxxv. 27 ; *v.* 17*a* as xxxv. 10, xxxvii. 14.

gether, how is the unity of the Psalm to be maintained? How can the poet in the same breath thank God for his deliverance, and complain that he is surrounded by troubles innumerable? *Vv.* 2-3 cannot synchronise with *v.* 12 : if the unity of the Psalm is to be preserved, *v.* 2 f. must describe the danger from which the Psalmist was delivered in the past, and *v.* 12 the fresh troubles which have fallen upon him since. Observe how a single word in P.B.V., A.V., R.V. obscures this. ' *Hath* put ' in *v.* 3 suggests what has just occurred, and so is in contradiction with *v.* 12 : we require aorists throughout *vv.* 1-3 : what is described in these verses is then thrown entirely into the past : *v.* 12 describes what is happening in the present ; and the two parts of the Psalms become perfectly consistent.

The Psalm is one of those in which the speaker *might* be not an individual, but Israel, as represented by its Godfearing members, and personified (so Cheyne, Bäthgen). The ' pit ' from which the speaker was rescued would in this case be the exile (cf. Lam. iii. 53-6, referred to above ; and with *v.* 3, cf.

Isaiah xlii. 10, xl. 5*a*, lii. 10*b*). The 'I' of the Psalms unquestionably sometimes denotes the nation (Ps. xliv., cii., cxviii.) ; and the figures and expressions could be more than paralleled from Lam. iii., where the speaker is certainly the nation. The first (and second) person singular is often used of a people or tribe even in Hebrew prose ; and Israel itself is frequently in the prophets personified as an individual ('when Israel was a child, then I loved him, and called my son out of Egypt,' Hos. xi. 1 ; ' O Lord, correct me, but with judgement, not in thine anger, lest thou bring me to nothing,' Jer. x. 24).[1] There is thus no objection in principle to this view of the Psalm : we have only to consider whether the expressions and language of the Psalm can naturally, and without forcing or artificiality, be understood of the nation. The explanation of the Psalm remains the same as if the speaker were an individual.

The Psalm thus portrays an *ideal* of obedience and spiritual service. A ready and

[1] See further instances cited in my *Introduction*, p. 366 f. (ed. 6-8, p. 389 f.).

STUDYING THE PSALTER

willing obedience, not to the ceremonial requirements of the Law, but to the moral and spiritual demands which God makes of His worshippers, is the best and truest return which a grateful heart can render for mercies received. As has been already pointed out, this is the teaching of all the great prophets; and here the Psalmist endorses and affirms it in his own person.

It has been remarked above that *vv.* 6-8*a*, as read in the LXX (with some slight variations), are quoted in Hebrews x. 5-7 with reference to Christ ('Wherefore when he cometh into the world he saith, Sacrifice and offering thou wouldest not,' etc.). It must be obvious that the Psalm, in its original intention, has no reference to Christ: it is some Old Testament saint, not Christ, who declares that it is his delight to do God's will; hence 'I am come' in *v.* 7 cannot refer to the Incarnation: if further proof were needed, it would be found in *v.* 12, where the Psalmist speaks of his 'iniquities,' which, except by most strained and unnatural exegesis, can be understood only of the iniquities which he

METHOD OF STUDYING THE PSALTER

has himself committed. It is, of course, perfectly true that parts of the Psalm are appropriate to Christ, and might well have been taken up by Him upon His lips ; but to argue from this fact that the Psalm was written with reference to Him, or that the entire Psalm is applicable to Him, is to confuse two things that are entirely distinct. A possible *application* of a Psalm is no guide to its *interpretation*, and cannot determine its original intention. Rather, the author of the Epistle to the Hebrews puts *vv.* 6-8*a* into Christ's mouth, not because the Psalm as a whole refers to Him, but because, as expressing a high ideal of obedience and spiritual service, these verses are, in the words of the present Dean of Ely, a ' fitting expression of the purpose of His life,' and of His perfect conformity to His Father's will. And so the Psalm is suitably appointed in the Anglican Church as one of the proper Psalms for Good Friday.

PSALM XXII

PSALM XXII

THE greatest and most striking of the 'Psalms of complaint,' or Psalms describing the sufferings of different godly men under the older dispensation. Here the speaker (1) expostulates with God for abandoning him to the scorn and derision of men (*vv.* 1-10) ; (2) pleads earnestly for help, describing alternately the virulence of his enemies, and his own pitiable condition (*vv.* 11-21) ; (3) assured suddenly of his deliverance, avows his purpose of proclaiming publicly his gratitude (*vv.* 22-26) ; and (4) ends by anticipating the far-reaching consequences of his deliverance, how God's kingdom will be extended, and His praises celebrated, in all the world (*vv.* 27-31). A study of the Psalm as a whole seems to show that the speaker can hardly be an individual as such, but an individual identifying himself with the nation at large, and speaking on its behalf : hence Bäthgen heads the Psalm with these words, *Israel's suffering and deliverance, a means to the conversion of the heathen.*

The Psalms which ought in particular to be compared with Psalm xxii. are Psalms lxix., lxxi. and cii. : of course, there are others which describe sufferings and expected deliverance (as vi., xxviii., xxxi., liv., lv.) ; but the Psalms that have been quoted contain closer and more noticeable resemblances : xxii., lxix. and cii. are constructed on the same model ; first the sufferings are described, then follows the outlook into the future, of similar scope and character (xxii. 1-21, 22-31 ; lxix. 1-21, 30-36 ; cii. 1-11, 15-22) ; of lxix. 32*b*. and xxii. 26*b*, one must be a reminiscence of the other, cf. also lxix. 33 with xxii. 24 : with xxii. 9-10 ; 11*a* ; 19*b* compare also lxxi. 5*b*, 6*a*, *b* ; 12*a* ; 12*b*, respectively. Of course, there are at the same time differences : thus in Psalm xxii. there is no allusion to the speaker's sin, as in lxix. 5, nor are there any imprecations as in lxix. 22-28 ; nor again is there any reference in it

XXII] STUDYING THE PSALTER

to an approaching restoration of exiles and re-building of Zion, as in lxix. 33, 35-36, and cii. 13-14, 16, 20-22.

The Psalmist begins by asking in pleading tones why God has forsaken him, and why his prayers for help bring him no relief : God's refusal to answer his prayers seems to him to be strangely inconsistent with His character—

1 My God, my God, why hast thou forsaken me,
   (being) far from helping me, and (from) the words of my roaring ?
2 O my God, I call by day, but thou answerest not ; and at night, but find no respite.
3 And (yet) thou art holy,
   O thou that art enthroned[1] upon the praises of Israel.

V. 1. *From helping me.* Hebrew, *from my salvation* or *deliverance* : see the note above on xl. 10. A very slight change (מְשׁוּעָתִי for מישעתי), i.e., ' being far from my

[1] Lit. *that sittest* ; but 'sit' in Hebrew, spoken of a king or of God, has usually the implication of being enthroned : cf. ii. 4, xxix. 10, xcix. 1, etc.

THE METHOD OF [PSALM

cry,' would improve the parallelism, and may well be the original reading.

Of my roaring. The Hebrew poets indulge sometimes in strong metaphors : in xxxii. 3, xxxviii. 8, also, the groans of a sufferer are spoken of as a lion's roar.

V. 3. God's *holiness* is manifested in *judgement*—in the destruction of sinners, and deliverance of His own faithful worshippers [1]; how comes it then that, being holy, He is deaf to the complaint of His persecuted servant ? He is enthroned on the praises of His people—their praises for past deliverances : has He ceased to give occasion for such praises to be uttered ? The speaker's continued sufferings seem to him a slur on God's attribute of holiness, and inconsistent with His character as one who delivers the righteous when they call upon Him, and

---

[1] See especially Ez. xxviii. 22 'Behold, I am against thee, O Zidon : and I will get me glory (Ex. xiv. 4) in the midst of thee ; and they shall know that I am Jehovah, when I execute judgements in her, and *show myself holy* in her.' Similarly *v.* 22, xx. 41, xxxviii. 16, 23, xxxix. 27.

XXII] STUDYING THE PSALTER

evokes from their hearts the praises of joy and thanksgiving.

Vv. 4–10. The fathers were delivered, he is deserted ; he is despised of all, and mocked : and yet God, who now forsakes him, had been his supporter from his birth ; he had been dependent on Him all his life.

4 In thee did our fathers trust ;
    they trusted, and thou didst deliver them.
5 Unto thee they cried, and escaped ;
    in thee did they trust and were not confounded.
6 But *I* am a worm, and no man ;
    a reproach of men, and despised of the people.
7 All they that see me make a mock at me ;
    they gape with the lip, they shake the head,[1] (saying,)
8 ' Commit (thyself) unto Jehovah ![2] let Him deliver him !
    let Him rescue him, seeing He delighteth in him ! '

---

[1] Gestures of derision : xxxv. 21, xliv. 14, cix. 25.
[2] Heb. *Roll* (it) *upon Jehovah*, i.e., Transfer, commit, thy cause to Him. The same figure, but with an object expressed, in xxxvii. 5 ' *Roll* thy way upon Jehovah,' and Prov. xvi. 3 ' *Roll* thy works upon Jehovah, and thy purposes shall be established.' LXX ἤλπισεν (hence Vulg. *speravit*), Jerome *confugit*, Pesh. *he trusted*, Matt. xxvii. 43 πέποιθεν (cf. P.B.V. *he trusted*), read presumably *gal* (3 pf.) for *gōl* (*imper.*),—though according to usage, the verb being transitive, *gālal* would have been expected

THE METHOD OF   [PSALM

9 For thou art he that caused (?)[1] me to burst forth[2]
   from the womb;

in the perf. (Böttcher, § 1118 (1); cf. G.-K. § 67 *aa, bb*),—
and paraphased. Wellh. would obviate the abrupt
change of person by reading יָגֵל 'let him commit.'
The omission of the object remains, however, in any
case, harsh; and נאלו for גל אל ' Jehovah is his redeemer!'
(Halévy, Cheyne formerly)—of course meant ironically
—is a very plausible emendation: the taunt would
be the more pointed, as in II. Isaiah Jehovah is repeatedly
called Israel's 'redeemer' (viz. from exile and suffering),
e.g. xli. 14, xlvii. 4.

[1] The transitive sense is uncertain.

[2] The word is used of the bursting forth of water
Job xl. 23 (of the Jordan: A.V., R.V. *swell*), xxxviii. 8
(of the sea, at the creation, pictured poetically as bursting
forth from the womb: A.V., R.V., *brake forth*), Mic. iv.
10 'Be in throes, and *burst forth* (A.V., R.V. *labour to
bring forth*), O daughter of Zion, like a woman in travail';
fig. of an ambush, bursting forth from its hiding-place,
Jud. xx. 33. Ps. lxxi. 6 is evidently based upon reminiscences of *vv.* 10, 9 here:—

Upon thee have I stayed myself from the belly:
   thou art he that severed me [or, hast been my
   rewarder] from my mother's bowels.

The doubtful word *gōzi*—found only here—rendered
he that severed me (cf. Aram. גזא, usually *to bereave*,
but occasionally *to cut off*), or *my rewarder* (as in Arabic,
and Christian Palestinian Aramaic)—differs very slightly
from the one rendered 'he that caused (?) me to burst
forth,' in Ps. xxii. 9. (*gōhi*).

STUDYING THE PSALTER

> thou madest me trust[1] (when I was) upon my mother's breasts.
> 10 Upon thee have I been cast from the womb;
> thou art my God from my mother's belly.

V. 6. For the figure of a worm, denoting something utterly despised and defenceless, compare Isaiah xli. 14 ' Fear not, thou worm, Israel ' (followed by promises of deliverance and victory). With *v*. 6*b* compare Isaiah xlix. 7 ' To him that is despised of men,[2] abhorred of the nation, a servant of rulers ' (of the ideal Israel).

Vv. 11–21. The Psalmist pleads for help still more earnestly. Jehovah is far off, and trouble is near: his enemies, like bulls, surround him with menacing mien: he is

---

[1] Or, reading with LXX. (ἐλπίς), Syr., Vulg. (*spes*), Jer., מבטחי for מבטיחי (really only a change of vocalisation; the poet's autograph would hardly have the first י in מבטיחי), (*thou wast*) *my trust*. Cf. Ps. lxxi. 6 ' the Lord Jehovah is *my trust* from my youth.' P.B.V. ' my hope ' (from the Vulg.) implies, of course, the same reading.

[2] Lit. *of soul*, i.e. heartily, intensely, despised: see for the usage Ps. xvii. 9 ' my enemies in *soul* ' = my greedy, deadly enemies; and cf., on the force of ' soul,' my *Parallel Psalter*, p. 460.

paralysed with fear, and brought to the point of death : like the troops of hungry and savage dogs with which every Oriental city and village still abounds, his foes come thronging around him, and—keeping up the figure—fly at his hands and feet, biting great holes in them : he is so emaciated that he can count his bones : his foes gloat upon the spectacle of his misery, and are only waiting for his death, that they may strip his body and divide his clothes between them.

11 Be not far from me ;[1] for trouble is nigh :
    for there is none to help.
12 Many bulls surround me :
    strong ones of Bashan[2] [3] close me in on every side.[3]

---

[1] Comp. the same words in lxxi. 12a.

[2] Bashan, on the East of Jordan, was famed for its rich pastures (cf. Jer. l. 19), and herds of fine cattle (cf. Deut. xxxii. 14, Ezek. xxxix. 18). 'Strong' (or, mighty) ones is a poetical expression sometimes for war-horses, as Jud. v. 22, sometimes for bulls, as here, l. 13, and lxviii. 30. LXX, reading רְשֵׁן for בָּשָׁן, have ταῦροι πίονες for 'bulls of Bashan' (so Vulg. *tauri pingues*),—and this is the origin of the '*fat* bulls of Bashan' of P.B.V.

[3] In the Heb. one word : cf. Jud. xx. 43 ('inclosed ... round about ').

XXII] STUDYING THE PSALTER

13 They open their mouth against me,
   (as) a ravening and a roaring lion.
14 I am poured out like water,[1]
   and all my bones are parted asunder :[2]
   my heart is become like wax ;
   it is melted[3] in the midst of my bowels.
15 My strength[4] is dried up like a potsherd ;
   and my tongue cleaveth to my gums ;
   and thou art laying me in the dust of death.
16 For dogs surround me :
   a company of evil-doers have inclosed me ;
   they have digged[5] my hands and my feet.

---

[1] Fig. for, am paralyzed with fear. Cf. Ezek. vii. 17 'and all knees shall *go into water*,' xxi. 7 [Heb. 12].

[2] The very framework of his body seems to give way.

[3] Fig. for, become weak and powerless through fear. Cf. Deut. xx. 8, Josh. ii. 11, *al.* In Josh. vii. 5 'melted and became as water.'

[4] Read probably, transposing two letters, *My palate.* Cf. Lam. iv. 4 'The tongue of the sucking child cleaveth to his palate for thirst.' Here, like 'cleaveth to my gums' in the next line, as an effect of fear.

[5] So LXX. (ὤρυξαν), Vulg. (*foderunt*) ; cf. Syr. בזעו, i.e. *cleft, pierced.* The Heb. text (כָּאֲרִי) can only be rendered *like a lion* (cf. Targ. 'biting *like a lion*'). Other versions also presuppose a verb : Aq. *they bound* (so Jerome, *vinxerunt*) : Symm. *as seeking to bind* (prob. reading כַּאֲרִי). There is no Heb. word like כאר meaning *to bind* ; but the Arab. כור means *to wind*

17 I can count all my bones :
   they[1] look (and) gaze upon me.[2]
18 They part my garments among them,
   and upon my vesture[3] do they cast lots.

The Psalmist, reduced thus to extremity, repeats more urgently his prayer for help, and entreats to be rescued from his relentless foes—

or *roll round*. Aq. is also reported to have rendered— presumably in his second edition — ᾔσχυναν : this implies a derivation from the Syr. *ka'ar*, *to disgrace*. LXX ὤρυξαν presupposes presumably בָּאֲרוּ (with an otiose א, like קאם, Hos. x. 14, and ראמה, Zech. xiv. 10), from כּוּר, a verb not otherwise found in Hebrew, but presupposed by מְכוֹרָה *origin*, Ez. xvi. 3, xxi. 35, xxix. 14, if this means properly a *place of digging* (cf. for the figure Is. li. 1), and in any case a possible by-form of כָּרָה, one of the ordinary Heb. words for 'dig,' used, for instance, of digging a well, or a pit (Gen. xxvi. 25, Ex. xxi. 33, Jer. xviii. 20). Or we might simply read כָּרוּ, the normal 3d. pers. plur. of כרה. In any case, however, the use of the word here is peculiar : for כרה does not mean to 'pierce' ; nor is it elsewhere construed except with an accusative of the cavity dug.

[1] I.e. my foes.

[2] Viz. with triumphant delight : cf. xcii. 11, cxii. 8, cxviii. 7.

[3] I.e. the long tunic, worn next the skin, which would be woven in one piece, and consequently be valuable only as a whole.

XXII]   STUDYING THE PSALTER

19 But thou, Jehovah, be not thou far off ;
    O my succour, haste thee to help me.[1]
20 Deliver my soul from the sword
    my only one [2] from the power [3] of the dog.
21 Save me from the lion's mouth,
    and from the horns of the wild-oxen [4]—thou
        hast answered (and delivered) [5] me !

In *v.* 21, if the text is right, the Psalmist, by a sudden impulse of faith, pictures his deliverance accomplished ; and instead of

[1] Comp. ' haste thee to help me ' in lxxi. 12*b*.

[2] Poet. for *my life*,—the one precious possession, which can never be replaced. So xxxv. 17. It is the word used of an only daughter, Jud. xi. 34.

[3] Heb. *hand* : often used figuratively (as ' from the hands of the sword,' Job v. 20).

[4] A fierce, untameable animal (see the description in Job xxxix. 9–12), with formidable horns (cf. Num. xxiii. 22, Dt. xxxiii. 17), the *Urus* of Caesar (*B.G.* vi. 28), now extinct. It is mentioned, under the same name *rîmu*, by the Ass. kings : Tiglath Pileser I. (*c.* 1100 B.C.), for instance, states that he hunted and killed four in the land of Mitanni (Schrader, *K.B.* i. 39), and brought back their horns and hides to the city of Asshur.

[5] The word ' answer ' is construed pregnantly, as is the case not unfrequently in Hebrew with other verbs construed with ' from ' ; e.g. ' to judge (and save) from,' Ps. xliii. 1 (see B.D.B. p. 578*a*).

'and from the horns of the wild-oxen answer (and deliver) me,' says ' and from the horns of the wild-oxen—thou hast answered (and delivered) me ! ' From this point all thought of the Psalmist's malicious assailants vanishes ; and the depth of despair is abruptly succeeded by the fulness of joy, and the thought of the happy and far-reaching consequences of his deliverance.

In *vv.* 22–31 the Psalmist develops these consequences. The change of tone is striking ; we may remember how, in Mendelssohn's well-known setting of the Psalm, it is effectively expressed by the change in the music from the minor to the major key of E.

First, then, he will proclaim God's goodness in a public act of thanksgiving, in which he bids all Israel take part (*vv.* 22–26) :

22 I will tell of Thy name unto my brethren ;
    in the midst of the congregation will I praise Thee :
23 ' Ye that fear Jehovah, praise Him ;
    ' all ye the seed of Jacob, glorify Him ;
    ' and stand in awe of Him, all ye the seed of Israel.

XXII]   STUDYING THE PSALTER

24 ' For He hath not despised nor abhorred the affliction [1]
   of the afflicted ; [2]
  ' neither hath He hid His face from him ;
  ' but when he called unto Him, He heard.'
25 From Thee (cometh) my praise in the great congregation :
   my vows will I pay in the sight of them that fear Him.
26 The humble shall eat and be satisfied :
   they shall praise Jehovah that seek after Him :
   let your heart live [3] for ever !

V. 22. The Hebrews regarded a ' name ' as the manifestation of a character : hence, ' Thy name ' means here ' all that Thou hast shown Thyself to be '—not, i.e., on this occasion only, but in general. By ' brethren ' the Psalmist means his compatriots. For ' in the midst of the congregation ' compare xxxv. 18, xl. 10, and xxvi. 12, lxviii. 26. In Psalm lxix. the parallel (*v.* 30) is, ' I will praise the name of God with a song, and magnify Him with thanksgiving.'

---

[1] LXX δέησιν, suggesting צעקה ' cry ' (for ענות— with צ fallen out after the preceding צ), which may be right ; notice the parallel in *v.* 24*c*.

[2] Or, *of the poor.* Cf. above, on Ps. lxxii. 2.

[3] I.e. let your failing spirits revive. See p. 170.

Vv. 23, 24. Here the Psalmist invites all Israel to join with him in praising Jehovah for His deliverance, ' Seed of Jacob,' as Isaiah xlv. 19, Jeremiah xxxiii. 26 ; ' seed of Israel,' as Isaiah xlv. 25, Jeremiah xxxi. 37. With ' despised ' compare the same word in lxix. 33, cii. 17.

V. 25. Jehovah, by delivering him, gives him occasion to praise Him ; the thank-offerings (Lev. vii. 16) which he had vowed to give, in the event of his deliverance (see Ps. lxvi. 13, 14 [P.B.V. 12]), he can now, therefore, gladly bring. The payment of vows is often mentioned in the Old Testament, as implying an answer to a prayer for deliverance (Ps. l. 14 f., lxi. 8, cxvi. 14, 18, Isa. xix. 21). Notice in P.B.V. the misleading ' of,' used here in its old sense of ' from ' (as in ' salvation is *of* the Jews,' ' God *of* God,' etc., in the Nicene Creed, and often) : in Ps. lxxi. 6, on the contrary, ' of ' in the modern sense of ' about ' is correct.

V. 26. The ' humble,'—i.e., as often in the Psalms, the pious worshippers of God [1]—will

---

[1] See, on the usage of the word, the writer's art. ' Poor ' in Hastings' *D.B.*

XXII] STUDYING THE PSALTER

now also be able to partake of, and enjoy, a eucharistic meal, such as always accompanied a ' peace-' or ' thank-'offering (Deut. xii. 17 f., xxvii. 7 ; Lev. vii. 15 f.), whether (on the analogy of Deut. xiv. 29, xxvi. 12[1]) as invited by the Psalmist, or as themselves delivered at the same time, and so able likewise to bring their thankofferings.   To ' eat,' of partaking of a sacrificial meal, as Genesis xxxi. 54, Exodus xviii. 12, xxiv. 11, xxxiv. 15 and Numbers xxv. 2 (in these two passages, in heathen worship, but the passages illustrate the ancient practice), 1 Sam. ix. 13. To 'eat and be satisfied ' is a common combination, Deuteronomy vi. 11, viii. 10, xi. 15, xiv. 29, xxvi. 12, Joel ii. 20, $al.$ Those who ' seek ' Jehovah, i.e. His devoted followers, may now unite in praising Him ; the hearts of all His worshippers, which have long been cast down, may also revive, and hope confidently for a continuance of happiness and freedom. For

[1] Though the reference here is not to a sacrificial meal, partaken of at the central sanctuary, but to the meals at which, according to Deuteronomy, the tithe, once in three years, was to be eaten locally by the poor of the district.

'live,' or 'revive' (the Hebrew is the same), compare—as David Kimchi did long ago—Genesis xlv. 27, 'And Jacob's spirit *revived*' (lit. *lived*), and the opposite in 1 Samuel xxv. 37 'And Nabal's heart *died* within him.' Notice the parallel in Psalm lxix. 32—

> The *humble* shall see, and be glad :
> Ye that *seek* after God, *let your heart live* (revive) !

Vv. 27–31. The speaker's outlook takes a wider range, embracing all mankind, and extending to future ages : the effect of his deliverance will be that *all* nations, through sucessive generations, will pay homage to Israel's God. It is a picture of the ideal future which the poet here draws—the future so often looked forward to and delineated by the prophets, in which peace and justice and true religion will prevail, sometimes in Israel, sometimes, as here, in the world at large. It is a specially noticeable feature of the present description that the advent of the ideal age is the consequence of the speaker's deliverance. Other Psalmists, when they look forward to deliverance after suffering, do not contemplate

XXII] STUDYING THE PSALTER

consequences extending beyond themselves (Ps. vi. 8–10, xxviii. 6–7, xxxi. 21, liv. 6–7, lvi. 12–13). But here the speaker is Israel; and the poet is writing under the influence of the great ideals of Deutero-Isaiah. Psalm cii. 15–22, where the gathering together of the nations to serve Jehovah is represented as a consequence of the restoration of Israel from exile, and of the rebuilding of Jerusalem, ought to be compared.

27 All the ends of the earth shall remember and turn
    unto Jehovah;
        and all the families of the nations shall worship [1]
        before Thee.
28 For the kingdom is Jehovah's;
        and He is ruler over the nations.
29 All the fat ones of the earth have eaten and wor-
    shipped;
        all that go down into the dust shall bend the knee
        before Him,
        and he that hath not kept his soul alive.
30 A seed shall serve him;
        it shall be told of the Lord unto the coming [2]
        generation.

---

[1] Heb. (as always) *bow down*.
[2] It is next to impossible that 'the generation' can

31 They[1] shall come and shall declare His righteousness
unto a people that shall be born, that He hath done
(it).

*V. 27. We have here a lyric echo (cf.
lxxxvi. 9, lxxxvii., cii. 15, 22) of the great
prophetic thought (Isa. ii. 2–4, Jer. xvi. 19, etc.)
of the future acceptance of Israel's religion by
the nations of the world. V. 28 states the
ground of this: because viz. Jehovah is by
right the sovereign of the nations, and the
time will come when this truth will be
recognised by them. The thought of Jehovah's
kingship over the world is prominent in later*

mean 'the next generation': notice the italic *next* in
R.V.: in xlviii. 17, lxxviii. 4, 6, cii. 18 the idea is expressed
by דור אחרון, lit. the 'after generation.' Most probably
יבא has dropped out before the following יבאו (*v.*
31*a*). Recent commentators indeed generally bring back
יבאו (in the form יבא) to the end of *v.* 30; but this
seems to shorten unduly the first line of *v.* 31. With
'come' (viz. to declare) in *v.* 31 comp. lxxi. 16, 'I will
come with the mighty acts of the Lord Jehovah (viz. in
my mouth); I will make mention of thy righteousness,
even of thine only.' Ps. lxxi. 18 seems indeed to contain
a parallel for this absolute use of דור: but there also it
can hardly be doubted that the text is in some disorder.

[1] I.e. the 'seed' and 'generation' of *v.* 30.

XXII] STUDYING THE PSALTER

writings : see especially Isa. lii. 7 *end* (hence Ps. xciii. 1, xcvi. 10, xcvii. 1), Psalm xlvii. 2, 8, Obadiah 21, Zech. xiv. 9.

V. 29. *All the fat ones of the earth*, i.e., those who are well nourished and in the full enjoyment of life, and also, it is no doubt implied, of prosperity, *have* [1] *eaten* (the perfect is the ' prophetic perfect,' describing a scene which the poet visualises, as if it were already present ; comp. e.g. Isa. ix. 2–6, xxxiii. 5) *and worshipped*—viz. again, as in *v.* 26, at a sacrificial meal, of which they will partake in token of homage. Moreover, not only those in the pride of life, but *those* also *who go down to the dust* and *he that hath not kept his soul alive*, i.e. those sinking into the grave, will *bow* (Ps. lxxii. 9, Isa. xlv. 23) *before Him*, and own His sway. *Have eaten* can be explained, as is done above, from usage (Exod. xviii. 12, xxiv. 11 ; cf. on *v.* 26) : still the thought

[1] Cf. Deut. xxxi. 20 ' when they shall have eaten, and satisfied themselves [above, *v.* 26, here], and *waxen fat* ' ; Ps. xcii. 14 (where ' full of sap ' is in the Heb. ' fat,' as here) ; and the fig. use of ' be made fat ' in Prov. xi. 25, xiii. 4, xxviii. 25.

comes in here abruptly ; and the emendation, made independently by Bruston in 1873, and by Bäthgen in 1880, which has been widely accepted (Nowack, Kirkp., Cheyne, *al.*), and which implies a very slight change in the Hebrew (אך לו ישתחוו for אכלו וישתחוו), is quite possibly right—

Unto Him all the fat ones of the earth shall *surely* bow down,

to which the following line forms an excellent parallel—

Before Him shall bend the knee all that go down into the dust.

The two classes of persons mentioned do not form a logical dichotomy ; but two representative classes of men are mentioned—those well nourished and prosperous, and those sinking into the grave—who, in the future which the Psalmist here anticipates, will alike acknowledge Jehovah's sway.

Vv. 30, 31. The children of the persons mentioned in *v.* 29 will serve Him ; and the story of the deliverance will thus be handed on to successive generations : cf., for the practice, Judges vi. 13, Psalm xliv. 1, lxxviii. 3, 4, Joel i. 3. The 'seed' means the immediate descendants of the persons mentioned in *v.* 29, and is equivalent to the 'coming generation' of the following line. This 'generation,' in its turn, recounts the story of Jehovah's doing to its successors : so that altogether it is pictured by the poet as handed on through three generations (*vv.* 29, 30, 31). Jehovah's 'righteousness' (*v.* 31) is that manifested in the deliverance of His servant and the discomfiture of his foes : compare xl. 9, 10, and in II. Isaiah (above, p. 145, note 1) ; and see Skinner in Hastings' *D.B.*, iv. 280*a*. In *v.* 31*b* 'done' is used absolutely, as sometimes elsewhere, in a full and pregnant sense which it is difficult to represent effectively in English : cf. xxxvii. 5 'Commit thy way unto Jehovah, and trust in Him, and *He* will *do* (or *act*)' : lii. 9 ; cxix. 126 ; Isaiah xliv. 23. With 'a people that shall be born' compare 'a people that shall be created,' also of a future generation, in Ps. cii. 18 (='an after generation').

For the construction in the Hebrew of $v.$ 29c, as rendered above, see G.K. § 155 n (b). It is difficult, however, to be sure of the exact sense of $v.$ 29. It is not certain how some of the terms used are to be understood: do the 'fat ones,' for instance, denote simply those in the vigour of life and strength? or does the expression imply also the collateral ideas of wealthy, self-sufficient, worldly, and impious, such as certainly were sometimes associated by the Hebrews with 'fatness' (see especially Job xv. 25-27; and cf. Deut. xxxi. 20, xxxii. 15, Jer. v. 29: on the other hand, to be 'made fat' is a blessing in Prov. xi. 25, xiii. 4, xxviii. 25)? The exact point of the antithesis between clauses a and b, c is not clear; there are also well-founded doubts whether the text is entirely in order. Thus $v.$ 29c appears to many scholars to be superfluous and to drag heavily after $v.$ 29b. so that Professor Cheyne (*Psalms*, 1888, p. 378) says, 'Sense and symmetry require us, with Hupfeld and Bickell, to attach the last clause of $v.$ 29 to $v.$ 30.' The absolute use of 'generation' in $v.$ 30b (without 'next' or 'coming'), as remarked above, is also strange. Hence various views have been taken of the meaning of the text, and various attempts have been made to emend it. Thus Cheyne in 1888 rendered and read—

29 Unto Him [1] all the fat ones of the earth shall surely bow down,
    all that have gone down into the dust shall bend the knee before Him;
    And as for him that kept not his soul alive,

---

[1] Adopting the emendation mentioned above (p. 174).

XXII] STUDYING THE PSALTER

30   his[1] seed shall be reckoned unto the Lord.
32 [2]To the coming generation[2] they shall declare His righteousness,
   to a people that shall be born, that He hath[3] done nobly.[3]

In the rendering given above, the meaning of *v.* 29 is that healthy and *dying*, i.e. all mankind, will alike own Jehovah's sway ; with this rendering the meaning of *v.* 29*a*, *b* is that living and *dead*—those in the full vigour of life and the feeble shades in the underworld—will alike own His sway (cf. for the thought Job xxvi. 5 R.V. marg. ; Phil. ii. 10). The participle, it is true, expresses quite regularly the present or approaching future (see Deut. *passim*) ; but in this and similar expressions it generally denotes in usage not those who *are* going down, but those who *have* gone down, to the grave (Ps. cxv. 17, Isa. xxxviii. 18, Ezek. xxvi. 20 (second time), xxxi. 14, 16) ; so that Professor Cheyne's rendering, if not necessary, is at least thoroughly legitimate.

Bäthgen in 1880, in a note in the *Studien und Kritiken*, pp. 756–9, proposed—

---

[1] זרעו for זרע. LXX ('*my* seed') express זרעי. יעבדנו ' shall serve Him ' is omitted, it being supposed that it was inserted to make sense after the disarrangement of the verses.

[2] לדור יבוא: יגידו for לדור ויגידו: יבואו (the verses being divided differently). LXX also have 'the coming generation.' Cf. p. 171 *n.* 2.

[3] Cheyne's rend. of the absolute use of עשה, noticed above.

29 Unto Him all the fat ones of the earth shall surely bow
        down,[1]
    before Him shall bend the knee all that go down
        into the dust.
    But my soul liveth unto Him,[2] (30) my seed [3] shall
        serve Him :
    it shall be told of the Lord unto the coming genera-
        tion.[1]
31 They shall declare His righteousness unto a people
        that shall be born,
    that He hath done (it).

The same renderings and readings were adopted by
Nowack in his revised edition of Hupfeld's Commentary
(1888) ; and they are also to be found in Bäthgen's own
Commentary (1892 ; ed. 2, 1904). Upon the view
expressed by them, those who 'go down into the dust'
in $v.$ $29b$ are the same as the 'fat ones of the earth' in $v.$
$29a$; and these are not merely men in the vigour of
health, but strong and prosperous heathen magnates,
who, as they sink into the grave, own implicitly thereby
the power of Jehovah : 'The great ones of the earth
sink into the dust : Israel, on the contrary, lives for its
God ; its individual members indeed perish, but their
descendants ($vv.$ 30, 31) perpetuate the worship of God,

---

[1] With the same emendations that have been mentioned before.

[2] I.e. ונפשי לו חָיָה (so LXX καὶ ἡ ψυχή μου αὐτῷ ζῇ)
for ונפשו לא חיה.

[3] זרעי for זרע, also with LXX. P.B.V. also has '*my
seed*.'

and through this uninterrupted service the community lives for ever to its God.'

Kirkpatrick (1891) read—

29 Surely Him[1] shall all earth's fat ones worship,
    before Him shall bow all they that go down into the dust.
    And as for him that hath not kept his soul alive,
30 his seed shall serve Him ;
    it shall be told of the Lord to the coming[2] generation.
31 And they shall declare His righteousness unto a people that shall be born
    that He hath done (it).

Kirkpatrick reads and interprets *v.* 29*a*, *b* as Bäthgen and Nowack do : the 'fat ones' are prosperous magnates, and *v.* 29*b* denotes what their fate nevertheless will be : earth's mightiest are but mortals, and must yield their homage to the King of kings. On the other hand (*vv.* 29*c*, 30*a*), the faithful Israelites who perish will leave a posterity behind them to serve Jehovah and perpetuate His praise.

But who is the speaker in the Psalm ? In spite of the title, certainly not David : we know pretty fully the circumstances of his life ; and we may be sure that he was never

---

[1] With the same emendations that have been mentioned before.

[2] With the emendation mentioned before.

reduced to straits such as are here described: the prophetical expectation of the conversion of the nations appears otherwise for the first time long afterwards, in the writings of Isaiah: the easy, flowing style points to a later age; and the Psalm is in parts palpably dependent upon Deutero-Isaiah. If the Psalm be a unity, also, the far-reaching consequences of the speaker's deliverance are much beyond what can be referred to David, or indeed to any single individual of the Old Testament dispensation. The speaker, it can hardly be doubted, is Israel. This, as Kautzsch observes,[1] is the only supposition which does justice to the triumphant close of the Psalm (v. 22 ff.), and makes it intelligible. The first person singular must not mislead us. In prose and poetry alike, Israel and other nations often speak, and are spoken to, or of, in the singular number. See, for instance, Lamentations i. 11c-16, 18–22, where the sufferings of the people, after the capture and sack of

[1] In the new edition of his *Die heilige Schrift des A.Ts.*, ii. p. 129.

XXII]   STUDYING THE PSALTER

Jerusalem by the Chaldaeans, are all described in the first person singular ;[1] and compare Psalm cii., where, at first sight, it seems as if the sorrows of an individual were being described (*vv.* 1–11, 23), but where a more careful reading of the Psalm shows that they are so contrasted with the rebuilding of Zion, the restoration of the nation, and the future gathering of peoples to serve Jehovah (*vv.* 13–22, 28), as to make it clear that the speaker is in reality the nation, and the conversion of nations is the effect of Israel's restoration. It was by reflexion on the character of Israel, in so far as in the persons of its more faithful members it suffered undeservedly, that the portrait of the suffering but righteous servant of God (Isaiah xlii., xlix., l., li. 13–liii. 12) arose ; and the speaker here is the same : Israel, and in particular faithful Israel, personified as an individual, persecuted but delivered, and its deliverance issuing in momentous conse-

[1] For other examples see Isa. xii. 1, 2, Jer. x. 19, 20, 24, Micah vii. 7–10, Hab. iii. 14 ; and comp. p. 150. In Ps. cxviii. also the first person undoubtedly denotes the nation.

quences for the world. It is remarkable that in Deutero-Isaiah God's servant, the ideal Israel, is described, in terms similar to those used here, as a worm, as one whom men despised and turned from in aversion, as persecuted and brought to the verge of the grave, but, nevertheless, with a great future before him (Isa. xli. 14, xlix. 7, l. 4–9, li. 7, lii. 14, liii. 2 f.)[1]: ideal Israel is, moreover, expressly called a 'light of the Gentiles' (xlii. 6, xlix. 6), and the restoration of Israel is represented as a signal manifestation of Jehovah's glory, producing a profound impression upon the nations who behold it, and disposing them to accept the religion of Israel (Isa. xl. 5, xlv. 6, lii. 10 ; cf. xlii. 1*b*, 3*b*, 4 [where ideal Israel is represented as establishing 'judgement,' i.e.

[1] For the figure (Ps. xxii. 9–10) of Israel being 'born,' and the object of God's care from its 'mother's womb,' cf. also Is. xliv. 2, xlvi. 3 (of the actual historic Israel), xlix. 1, 5 (of ideal Israel).

It may be deemed an objection to this interpretation of the Psalm, that in *v.* 22 the speaker is represented as addressing his 'brethren.' It must, however, be remembered that in II. Isaiah, also, though the same term is used to describe both the actual, historic Israel (as xli.

XXII] STUDYING THE PSALTER

religion,[1] in the earth], xlv. 23, li. 4, lxvi. 23). The teaching of the prophets often finds in the Psalms a lyrical echo : in Psalms xciii., xcvi., xcvii., xcviii., for instance, the thoughts of hope and deliverance expressed by Deutero-Isaiah are thus echoed ; in Psalm xxii. the thoughts echoed are those of persecution and suffering, of deliverance and the consequences following from it. The Psalmist, a godly Israelite himself, speaks in the person of the nation of which he is a member ; and on the

---

8-9, xlii. 19-20), and the ideal Israel (as xlii. 1-4, xlix. 1-9), yet ideal Israel is sometimes set over against the actual Israel, and sharply distinguished from it (comp. my *Isaiah : his life and times*, pp. 175-8 ; Skinner, *Isaiah*, vol. ii. pp. xxxiii.-iv., xxxvi., 235-6). This is notably the case in xlix. 5-6 ; it is also the case in liii. 1-6, where (at least as the passage is usually understood) the repentant Israelites reflect upon their previous misconception of the servant's character and work. The analogy of these passages sufficiently justifies the distinction implied in *v. 22*, if the speaker be Israel, between Israel and his ' brethren.'

[1] See Skinner's note on Is. xlii. 1 in the *Camb. Bible*, or Whitehouse's in the *Century Bible*. ' Judgement ' in Jer. v. 4, 5 (A.V., R.V.) has the same meaning : see my *Book of the Prophet Jeremiah*, p. 344 f.

basis of his own and his nation's sufferings, constructs a ' mosaic of suffering, to represent the woes of a faithful community, abandoned by God to their cruel foes ' (Briggs, p. 190). The exact situation we do not know : but it must have been at some time after the return from Babylon, when misfortune and the hostility of envious neighbours combined to make the outlook dark, and fill Israel with the gloomiest apprehensions. The expressions need not be all understood literally, any more than many of those in Lamentations iii. or Job xvi. In Lamentations iii. we read, for instance ($v.$ 4) ' My flesh and my skin He hath worn out ; He hath broken my bones,' ($v.$ 13) ' He hath made the shafts of His quiver to enter into my reins,' ($v.$ 16) ' He hath broken my teeth with gravel stones, He hath covered me with ashes,' and in Job xvi. ($v.$ 13) ' His archers compass me round about, He cleaveth my reins asunder, and doth not spare, He poureth out my gall upon the ground.' These and many other passages show clearly that the language of Hebrew poetry is often not to be understood literally. The really striking

XXII]   STUDYING THE PSALTER

thought in Psalm xxii. is that of the world-wide consequences attached to Israel's deliverance ; but this is a thought closely akin to what is expressed in Deutero-Isaiah (xlix. 6 f.).

It is thus not an actual individual, it is faithful Israel, speaking as an individual, who is persecuted and delivered ; and it is Israel's salvation which brings with it these far-reaching consequences affecting humanity at large. This view of the Psalm enables us to understand better than we could otherwise do its application to Christ. Christ is the ideal representative of Israel, the Man in whom the genius of Israel found its truest and fullest expression ; the righteous servant of II. Isaiah is a prefigurement of Him ; and the ideal both of the prophet and of the Psalm was fulfilled by Him. And so, though the Psalm is no *prediction* of the sufferings of Christ—for the intensely personal character of the description shows that they spring from, and reflect, the personal experiences of the writer and his faithful compatriots—yet the sufferings of godly Israel, so pathetically described in it, were realised by Him in His person ; while

METHOD OF STUDYING THE PSALTER

the glorious hopes for the future, with which the Psalm closes, foreshadow remarkably the blessed consequences of the life and death of Christ. The bringing of the world to a knowledge of God, set forth in the Psalm as a consequence of Israel's deliverance, was in any case conditioned by Israel's continued existence as a nation ; the ground was prepared for it by various events taking place in the centuries between the restoration and the birth of Christ—for instance, by the diffusion of Jews in the world, and the translation of the Old Testament into Greek : but the religion of Israel, in order to become a universal religion, had in many respects to be developed and transformed ; and these necessary changes were effected only as a consequence of the life and work of Christ.

PSALM XVI

PSALM XVI

A PRAYER for God's protecting care, based on the Psalmist's consciousness of the close communion with God which he enjoys, and of which nothing, he feels, can ever deprive him.

V. 1 is the prayer; *vv.* 2-4 state the ground of the Psalmist's assurance. Jehovah is his sole good, the sole source of his happiness; his only delight is in the company of the faithful; with apostates he will have no fellowship.

1 Keep me, O God: for I have taken refuge in thee.
2 I have said[1] unto Jehovah, 'Thou art my Lord;
   'all[2] my welfare (dependeth) upon thee.

---

[1] So Sept., Vulg., Syr. (cf. xxxi. 14, cxl. 6). The pointed Hebrew text has, *Thou* (fem.) *hast said*, implying an improbable ellipse of 'O my soul.' Comp. the same omission of the final י in the 1st pers. sing. of the perfect in cxl. 13, 1 Kings viii. 48, Ez. xvi. 59, Job xlii. 2 (in which cases, however, the omission is corrected in the Qrê).

[2] So, reading בְּלָּהּ for בַּל (כל alone, which has been

THE METHOD OF [PSALM

3 'As for the holy ones that are in the land,
'they are the nobles in whom is all my delight.'[1]

---

suggested, is not Hebrew). Lit. 'my welfare, all of
it,' emphatic for 'all my welfare' : see, for examples
of the usage, Ps. viii. 8, lxvii. 4, 6, 2 Sam. ii. 9, Isa. ix.
8, Mic. i. 2, ii. 12, Hab. ii. 6, and *Lex.* s.v. כל **1d** (p.
481*b*). For על = (rests, or is dependent,) *upon*, cf.
Jud. xix. 20, Ps. vii. 11 [Engl. 10 : see Kirkpatrick's
note], lxii. 8 [Engl. 7] ; *Lex.* p. 753c). Another suggestion (Houbigant, Hitzig, Duhm) is to read בל בלעדיך
for בל עליך, i.e. 'is not *apart from* or *without,
thee:* cf. Symm. οὐκ ἔστιν ἄνευ σοῦ ; Jer. 'non est
sine te ' ; Targ. ' is not given *except from thee* (בר מינך) ' ;
and for בלעדי *apart from, without* (χωρίς, ἄνευ), Gen. xli.
44. Either of these emendations would express what
seems clearly to be the general idea intended, viz. that
the Psalmist depends for his happiness upon God. Beyond ' (R.V.) is a doubtful paraphrase of על ; and ' is
not *in addition to* (Gen. xxxi. 50) thee ' is not a natural
way of expressing the idea ' is to be found wholly in
thee.'

[1] So, with a very slight change (אדירי for ואדירי),
and removing the *athnach* from המה to בארץ. אשר בארץ חמה
is incorrect Hebrew for ' who are in the land ' ;
this might be either אשר בארץ or אשר המה בארץ (Gen.
ix. 3, Num. ix. 13, xiv. 8, 27) ; but the pronoun in such cases never stands at the end, except after
a negative (as Gen. vii. 2, xvii. 12, Num. xvii. 5). See
my *Tenses,* §§ 198 *Obs.*, 199 *Obs ;* and *Lex.* הוא **2c, 3c,**

XVI]   STUDYING THE PSALTER

4 Their sorrows are multiplied that choose[1] another
  (God) ;
  their drink-offerings of blood will I not pour out,
  neither take up their names upon my lips.

1. *I have taken refuge.* The figure is one
of those expressive ones which we find in the
Psalms : he has taken refuge in God, as from
storm, or wind (Isa. iv. 6, xxv. 4), or stress of

המה **2c, 3c.** For the *st. c.* אדירי before the relative
clause cf. Ps. lxv. 5, Job xxix. 2 ; and see G.–K. § 130*d*.

[1] So, reading בחרו for מהרו : ב and מ are often
confused in Hebrew MSS., and the versions ; see my
Notes on Samuel, p. lxviii. (where many more instances
might have been cited). מהר is a most uncertain
word. It occurs nowhere else in a sense suitable here :
R.V. ' exchange [Jehovah] for another God ' depends
on the questionable assumption that מהר has the sense
of המיר ; besides, not only is there no ' for ' in the
Hebrew, but even granting that it had that sense, we
should expect as its accusative, not the object *taken*
in exchange, but, as in other cases, the object *given*
in exchange, i.e. Jehovah : cf. Jer. ii. 11 ' my people
have changed their glory *for* that which doth not profit '
(A.V., R.V.) ; Ps. cvi. 20 R.V. (' changed their glory
for the likeness of an ox that eateth grass ') ; Hos. iv.
7 (render similarly ' change *for* ' : A.V., R.V., incon-
sistently, ' change *into*,' which would be ל, not ב ;
for the ב, see *Lex.* p. 90, **3**).

foes (Ps. lxi. 3) ; he has confided himself to Him ; and on this ground he craves His protection. Both the word and the cognate subst. 'refuge' are very common in the Psalms (see my *Parallel Psalter*, p. 454) : the paraphase 'put trust' obliterates the metaphor, conceals the connexion with the subst. 'refuge,' and suggests an illusory connexion with the ordinary word for 'trust.' Comp. the note above, on ii. 12 (pp. 66 f.).

2. *Thou art my Lord* — my master or sovereign, to whose service I am devoted : *all my welfare* (for this sense of טובה, lit. *good*, see xxv. 13, cvi. 5, Job ix. 25, xxi. 13 [A.V. *wealth* (=*weal*), R.V. *prosperity*, etc.] *dependeth upon thee* : Thou art the sole source of my happiness.

3. The Psalmist proceeds to express his regard for character, above mere position or nobility of birth : the true nobles, in whose society he delights, are not the wealthy or the powerful, but those who realise Israel's ideal character of 'holiness' (Ex. xix. 6, Deut. xiv. 2, etc.) : with apostates, on the contrary, he will have no dealings ; he will not join in their

XVI]   STUDYING THE PSALTER

unholy offerings (cf. Is. lxv. 4), or take up
upon his lips (cf. Ex. xxiii. 13, Hos. ii. 17)
the names of their gods.

Drink-offerings of blood. Some heathen rite
is doubtless referred to ; we do not know
exactly what. The allusion may be to liba-
tions of blood offered by apostate Israelites
instead of wine and oil.

5 Jehovah is the share of my portion, and my cup :
    thou holdest fast [1] my lot.
6 The measuring-lines are fallen unto me in pleasant
    places ;[2]
    yea, I have a goodly heritage.[3]

---

[1] So, reading תּוֹמֵךְ for תּוֹמִיךְ, which is a *vox nihili*
in Hebrew.

[2] Lit. *in pleasantnesses.*

[3] Heb. *my heritage* [read נחלתי for נחלת:
G.-K. § 80*g*] *is fair* (so A.V., m.) *unto me.* Both the
verb שפר and its derivatives are very rare in Hebrew
(Gen. xlix. 21, Job xxvi. 13 (see R.V. m.), Jer. xliii. 10
R.V. m.) ; but it is common in Aramaic (both Targums
and Syriac), where it means not only *to be fair, beautiful,*
in a literal sense, but also *to seem fair* or *good* to ; and
it occurs in this latter sense in Dan. iv. 2 (Aram. iii. 32),
vi. 1 (Aram. 2), iv. 27 (Aram. 24),—in iv. 27 (where it
is rendered, ' be *acceptable* to '), followed, as here, by
עַל. Here it is used probably in its Aramaic sense, the

Jehovah, on the contrary, is the Psalmist's apportioned share, and his cup. The figures are derived partly from the distribution of land among a body of settlers, partly from a banquet at which every guest receives in course his share of refreshment.

For ' portion ' (חלק) in the sense of a portion of land, see Josh. xiv. 4, xv. 13, xviii. 5, 7, etc. ; and in the same spiritual sense, of Jehovah, as here, Ps. lxxiii. 26, cxix. 57, cxlii. 5, Lam. iii. 24, Jer. x. 16=li. 19.[1] The figure implies that the ' portion ' is one which the Psalmist has received (from God), not one which he has chosen himself. ' Cup ' is used elsewhere also in a figurative sense (Ps. xxiii. 5). ' The sense is, Jehovah is the portion which has been assigned to me to satisfy my thirst. The

meaning being not ' is beautiful,' but ' is fair, goodly, pleasing.' On the form מְנָת see Delitzsch on Ps. xi. 6, or G.-K. § 95 n.

[1] In Num. xviii. 20, where Jehovah says to Aaron, ' I am thy *portion* and thine inheritance,' the reference is merely to the altar-perquisites and other sacred dues, which formed the maintenance of the priests. ' Portion and inheritance ' in Dt. x. 9, xviii. 1 (cf. 2, Josh. xiii. 14, 33, xviii. 7) has a similar meaning.

desires and necessities of man's higher life are often represented by hunger and thirst, but especially by thirst as the keener and subtler appetite. Thus we read of a thirst for God's word (Am. viii. 11, 12); but especially the longing of the soul for personal communion with God is spoken of as the thirsting of the soul for Him (Ps. xli. 2, lxiii. 1). Conversely the joys of this fellowship are a " river of delights " flowing from the fountain of life which is with God, and from which He gives His people to drink (Ps. xxxvi. 8, 9).'[1] And here Jehovah Himself, as the full satisfaction of the Psalmist's spiritual being, is called his ' cup.'

Thou holdest fast my lot, so that no one can snatch it from me. ' Lot,' meaning properly the ' lot ' cast (Lev. xvi. 8), is also used metaphorically of the *land allotted* (Jud. i. 3 *al.*); here fig. (cf., of misfortune, Is. xvii. 14, Jer. xiii. 25) of the lot in life which the Psalmist enjoys, i.e. of the blessings, spiritual and

---

[1] W. R. Smith, in an interesting article on this Psalm in the *Expositor*, vol. iv. (1876), p. 348.

material alike, which follow from Jehovah's being his 'portion,' and 'cup.'

6. The '(measuring-) lines' and the 'inheritance' carry on the figure of the 'share of my portion' in *v.* 5. For 'line,' in the derived sense of the territory measured by the line, see Josh. xvii. 5 lit. 'And there fell ten *lines* to Manasseh,' and 14 'Wherefore hast thou given me as an inheritance, one *lot* [cf. *v.* 5*b*, here], and one *line* ?'

In pleasant places (lit. *pleasantnesses*). Cf. Job xxxvi. 11 (cited below, on *v.* 11), where the Hebrew word is the same. *Heritage* or *inheritance* (the same word in Hebrew) is elsewhere also used figuratively of a person's lot in life : e.g. Job xx. 29, xxvii. 13, Is. liv. 17. The reference might be to the outward prosperity and security, which accompany Jehovah's fellowship (Cheyne, Bäthgen) ; but the context (cf. *v.* 5*a*) favours the more general view that the 'inheritance' is 'the share which he has obtained among the spiritual joys of God's presence' (W. R. Smith). Or, still more probably, perhaps, a sharp distinction ought not to be drawn ; and in *v.*

XVI]   STUDYING THE PSALTER

6a, b, as in v. 5b, spiritual and material satisfactions alike are contemplated by the Psalmist.

7. In the joyful remembrance that he has such a possession, the Psalmist breaks out into a strain of thanksgiving—

7 I will bless Jehovah, who hath given me counsel;
    yea, in the nights my reins admonish me.
8 I have set Jehovah continually before me:
    because he is at my right hand, I shall not be moved.

Given me counsel; **viz.** in my course of life. Cf. lxxiii. 24 'Thou guidest me with thy counsel.' The 'reins,' i.e. the kidneys (Lat. *renes*), were in Hebrew psychology regarded as the springs of *feeling*; hence, when God is said to try, or see, the 'hearts and reins,' it is implied that he is cognizant of man's emotions and affections, not less than of his thoughts (which were regarded as having their seat in the heart).[1] Comp. vii. 9, xxvi. 2, Jer. xi. 20, xvii. 10, xx. 12; also Ps. lxxiii. 21, Jer. xii. 2, Prov. xxiii. 16. Thus the meaning here is that, at night time, the time of quiet meditation and reflection (cf. xlii. 8, lxxvii. 6, xcii. 2;

[1] Comp. the note on Ps. xl. 6 (pp. 140 f.).

also iv. 4, lxiii. 6), the emotions, or impulses, of his own breast (as we might now say) move him to respond to the Divine counsel, and follow its guidance.

8. His eye is ever fixed towards Jehovah; and conscious that, as he looks to Him, he is secure in having Him ever at his right hand as his champion and helper (cx. 5, cxxv. 5), he exclaims with confidence, *I shall not be moved*, i.e. not be disturbed in my prosperity,—in the 1st or 3rd person, a common expression in the Psalms to denote material security: x. 6, xv. 5, xxi. 7, xxx. 6, xlvi. 5, lxii. 2, 6, cxii. 6; cf. also xiii. 4, xciii. 1, xcvi. 10 (in these two passages, of the *social* order of the world being undisturbed, in consequence of Jehovah's assumption of sovereignty), civ. 5, cxxv. 1. Is. xl. 20, xli. 7, where it is used of an idol being displaced, and Deut. xxxii. 25, Ps. xxxviii. 16, xciv. 18 (A.V., R.V., in these passages *slide* or *slip*), where it is used of the foot *giving way* (fig. for falling into adversity), shew the sense in which 'be moved' is to be understood.

9–11. With this assurance of Jehovah's

XVI] STUDYING THE PSALTER

protecting power, his heart and spirit exult : he not only lives a life of undisturbed material felicity, but also anticipates the enjoyment of spiritual communion with God, unbroken even by death.

9 Therefore my heart is glad, and my glory rejoiceth :
    my flesh also dwelleth in safety.
10 For thou wilt not leave my soul to Sheol ;
    thou wilt not suffer thy godly one to see the pit.
11 Thou makest me to know the path of life :
    in thy presence [1] is fulness [2] of joys ;
    in thy right hand there are pleasures for ever.

9. *Glory* is a poetical expression for the highest and most honourable part of man, his immaterial spirit ; so Gen. xlix. 6, Ps. xxx. 12, lvii. 8 (= cviii. 1), and probably vii. 5.[3] His *flesh* also *dwelleth in safety*—an

[1] Lit. *beside thy face.* So xxi. 6, cxl. 13.

[2] Lit. *satiety*, said properly of food ; see the same word in Ex. xvi. 3 ('when we did eat bread *to the full*'), Ps. lxxviii. 25 ('sent them food *to the full*').

[3] This is the generally accepted view. It is, however, possible that we should, both here and in the other passages quoted, vocalise (as the Sept. did in Gen. xlix. 6) כְּבֵדִי, i.e. 'my *liver*' : so e.g. Cheyne in *Enc. Bibl.* s.v. LIVER, and Skinner, in his recently published

expression often used of undisturbed security in Palestine (Deut. xxxiii. 12, 28, Jer. xxiii. 6, xxxiii. 16, Prov. i. 33). 'Flesh' is parallel with 'heart' and 'glory' (i.e. 'spirit') here, as with 'soul' in lxiii. 1, and 'heart' in lxxiii. 26, lxxxiv. 2; it 'does not denote the dead corpse, but the living organism in and through which the soul works; together with heart or soul, it makes up the whole man' (Kirkpatrick). The verse thus describes how fellowship with Jehovah guarantees both inward joy and outward security; his spirit rejoices, his body is secure. The rend. of P.B.V., A.V., *shall rest in hope*, 'beautiful and suggestive as it is, is thus inaccurate and misleading' (Kirkpatrick); the words

commentary, in Gen. l.c. The combination of ideas may at first sight seem strange: but in itself there is nothing more remarkable in the liver being regarded as the seat of mental impulses or affections than there is in the kidneys or bowels being so regarded, as they unquestionably were by the Hebrews. The corresponding word in Assyrian, *kabittu*—which, however, is not found with the actual meaning 'liver'—has regularly the sense of *Gemüth*, *mind*, and is said to brighten, rejoice, etc. In English we could paraphrase by 'bosom.'

do not mean that the flesh after death will rest in the grave in hope, but that the Psalmist, while yet alive, dwells in confidence and security, without fear of danger or death.

10. For he feels confident that he will not be abandoned to Sheol, not surrendered by Jehovah, so as to experience the terrors of the huge dark cavern, deep down below the surface of the earth (in the ' lowest parts of the earth,' Ezek. xxvi. 20, xxxi. 14, 16, 18, xxxii. 18, 24, Ps. lxiii. 9 : cf. lxxxvi. 13 R.V.m., lxxxviii. 6), and its waters (Job xxvi. 5), where impenetrable darkness reigned (Job x. 21–2), and where the voice of praise was hushed (vi. 5, xxx. 9, lxxxviii. 10–12, cxv. 17, Is. xxxviii. 18), which the Hebrews believed to be the final ' house of meeting for all living ' (Job xxx. 23 R.V.m.). *To see the pit* (so R.V.m. ; Hebrew *sháḥath* ; not *corruption*, as A.V., R.V.), as xlix. 9 : elsewhere to ' go down to the pit ' is said (xxx. 19, Job xxxiii. 24 ; and with another word, *bõr*, for ' pit,' xxviii. 1, lxxxviii. 4, Ez. xxvi. 20, etc.) : conversely, when a person escapes mortal danger, he is said to be ' kept back,'

'brought back,' 'brought up,' or 'redeemed' from it (Job xxxiii. 18, 30, Ps. ciii. 4, Jon. ii. 6 : cf., with 'Sheol' and *bōr*, Ps. xxx. 3). The hope which the Psalmist expresses is thus not that he will rise again, but that he *will not die*. By *thy godly one* he naturally means himself. If the plural (which is read by the official Hebrew text, and many MSS.) is correct, other devout Israelites, like-minded with himself, will be included ; so that the various reading does not substantially affect the sense. The official Hebrew margin, and the majority of MSS., however, as well as all the ancient versions, have the singular, which agrees better with the context. The term 'godly (*lit.* kindly) one' is used often in the Psalms—and occasionally also besides— to denote the pious Israelite : see my *Parallel Psalter*, p. 443 f.

11. The Psalmist's sense of superiority to death is here further drawn out. *Thou makest me to know*—pointest out to me (cxliii. 8)—*the path of life*. The expression occurs more than once in the Proverbs, where it is opposed to the path which leads to death

XVI] STUDYING THE PSALTER

and Sheol, as ii. 18 f., ' Her house (the house of the 'strange woman') inclineth unto death, and her tracks unto the shades ; None that go to her return again, neither do they attain to the *paths of life* ' ; v. 5 f. ' Her feet go down to death, her steps take hold on Sheol : Lest thou make level[1] *the path of life*, her tracks totter, and thou knowest it not ' ; xv. 24 ' *The path of life* is upwards for the wise, in order to depart from Sheol beneath ' : cf. xii. 28 ' In the *path* of righteousness is *life*, and her pathway is no-death.' In these passages ' life ' means more than merely animal life : it means, or implies, a virtuous and happy life ; [2] in the Psalm

---

[1] Fig. for, *free from hindrances*, and so step easily upon. Elsewhere lit. (Ps. lxxviii. 50 R.V. m. ' He *levelled* a way for his anger ') ; or fig. for, to *make passable* in a general sense (Prov. v. 21), to *free from hindrances*, whether material (Is. xxvi. 7 ' evenly [lit. *into an even one ;* G.–K. § 117 *ii*] dost thou *level* the path of the just '), or moral (Prov. iv. 26 ' make *level* the path of thy feet ').

[2] For the idea of ' life ' in the Book of Proverbs, comp. such passages as iii. 18 (wisdom a ' tree of life ' to those who lay hold of her) ; iv. 13 (' instruction,' or moral

it means, or implies, something more even than this, but still something less than the life hereafter of the N.T. ; it is a life of happiness, brightened by a sense of God's presence and favour, a life, therefore, of which it may be hoped that it will not be interrupted by death, but of which this is not expressly affirmed. And so the Psalmist continues, *in thy presence* (viz. during the present earthly life (*is fulness of joys*—joys springing from a sense of God's favour, and from spiritual fellowship with Him ; *in thy right hand there are pleasures* (lit. *pleasantness*) *for ever,*— pleasures, that is, abidingly in God's hand, and ever ready to be dispensed by Him, as from an inexhaustible source : cf., for the figure, Prov. iii. 16 ' Length of days is *in her*

discipline, a man's ' life ') ; viii. 35 (whoso findeth wisdom findeth ' life ') ; x. 11 (' The mouth of the righteous is a fountain of life '); xiii. 12 (' Hope deferred maketh the heart sick, But when the desire cometh, it is a tree of life ') ; xvi. 22 (understanding a ' fountain of life '). Life in these passages is more than merely animal life ; it includes higher elements dependent upon a mental or moral state—wisdom, or righteousness, or inward satisfaction.

XVI]   STUDYING THE PSALTER

right hand ; in her left hand are riches and honour.'[1] As the context shews, the 'pleasures' meant are blessings given by God, especially the delights which are to be found only in Him, in contrast to fleeting and unsatisfying worldly joys. Comp. the same word—except that the form is there the fem.—in Job xxxvi. 11 'If they hearken and serve him, they spend their years in good (i.e. in prosperity), and their days in *pleasantness*,'[2] —where, however, material prosperity seems to be what is principally in the poet's mind.

The idea of a future life is in the O.T. only *nascent*. The ordinary belief on the subject of a future life, shared by the ancient Hebrews, was, not that the spirit after death ceased to exist, but that it passed into the underworld, 'Sheol,' the 'house of meeting for all living,' without any distinction between good and bad (Job xxx. 23), where it entered upon a

[1] The rendering '*at* thy right hand' is contrary to idiom, and incorrect.

[2] So R.V. m. 'Pleasures' suggests a hedonism that is not intended.

shadowy, half-conscious existence, devoid of interest and occupation, forgotten by God, and cut off from His hand (Ps. lxxxviii. 5 'Like the slain that lie in the grave, whom thou rememberest no more, and they are cut off from thy hand'), and not worthy of the name of 'life': 'For Sheol doth not praise thee, death doth not celebrate thee; they that go down into the pit do not hope for thy faithfulness' (Is. xxxviii. 18). But the darkness which thus shrouded man's hereafter was not unbroken in the O.T.: and there are *three* lines along which the way is prepared in it for the fuller revelation brought by the Gospel. There is, firstly, the limitation (Is. lxv. 22), or the abolition (Is. xxv. 8), of the power of death, set forth by the prophets in their vision of a glorified, but earthly, Zion of the future. There is, secondly, the conviction uttered by individuals that their close fellowship with God implies and demands that they will themselves be personally superior to death (Pss. xlix. 15, lxxiii. 24, 26, Job xix. 26). And thirdly, there is the idea of a resurrection, which gradually emerges

XVI] STUDYING THE PSALTER

in the Old Testament.[1] Ps. xvi. stands on the same level as Pss. xlix. and lxxiii. In none of these Psalms is the hope more than a 'postulate of faith,' a 'splendid hope, a personal and individual conclusion';[2] it is no generally accepted article of belief. The Psalmist does not speak explicitly of a future life (for v. 11 does not refer to it at all[3]); but he expresses the hope of superiority over death, grounded on the close personal relation in which he himself stands towards God, and which he cannot believe will be interrupted by death. The hope in Pss. xlix. and lxxiii. is based on the same ground: in contrast to those whose lives are devoted to the world, the writer of each of these Psalms has a conviction that God will 'take' him, and admit

[1] See, on the gradual growth in Israel of the belief in a future state, Dr. Burney's excellent *Four Lectures on Israel's Hope of Immortality*, 1909 (in the O.T., the Apocrypha, and Apocalyptic writings), and the present writer's *Sermons on Subjects connected with the O.T.*, pp. 72-98 (in the Book of Enoch and the Targums).

[2] Kirkpatrick, *The Psalms*, p. lxxviii.

[3] Or, at least, does not certainly refer to it: cf. Kirkpatrick, p. 78.

him to some greater bliss. But in the full sense of the words used, the hope of Ps. xvi. remained an unrealized ideal. The Psalmist suffered the lot of all other men. The Psalm is thus 'Messianic,' not in being a prediction of Christ's resurrection,—for it is plain that the feelings and hopes expressed in it are those of the Psalmist himself, or, at most, if the plural in *v.* 10 be the original reading, of himself and other like-minded godly Israelites,— but in expressing an *ideal*—a hope of superiority to death—which transcended experience, and was fully realized only by Christ. Even by Him, however, the hope was not realized literally, but only in substance; for Christ did, in the literal sense of the words, 'see the pit.' It is difficult not to think that the application of the words to Christ found in Acts ii. 25-31, xiii. 35-37 was facilitated by the mistranslations of the Septuagint ('shall dwell in hope,' 'wilt not leave my soul in Hades,' and 'to see corruption'). But the Apostles used arguments of the kind usual at the time, and such as would seem cogent both to themselves and to their contemporaries. As Mr.

XVI]   STUDYING THE PSALTER

Edghill says,[1] ' To his [St. Peter's] readers who took for granted the Davidic origin of the Psalter, and who agreed as a matter of course that the Messiah would be the Son of David, such illustrations would have carried considerable force. St. Peter shared their beliefs ; he and his hearers were on common ground ; and it was to increase their faith that he pressed home the witness of the Old Testament scriptures. It does not follow that the ' proofs ' possess for us the same value as they did for the men of that generation. St. Peter had in view the conversion of his own contemporaries ; and to secure that end he employed the arguments which he believed to be true, and knew to be effective.' The Psalm contains, like the other similar passages referred to above, a great declaration of the faith and hope of an Old Testament saint : it expresses also an *ideal*, both of fellowship with God, and of superiority to death : but, when we study it in itself, and consider it carefully in its original import, we see that *v*. 10 will not support the argument

[1] *Evidential Value of Prophecy*, p. 495 f.

which the Apostles built upon it, and that the Psalm cannot be appealed to, in the way in which they appealed to it, as a proof of the resurrection of Christ.

SERMONS ON THE PSALMS
PSALM CIX

PSALM CIX

Let there be no man to pity him,
  nor to have compassion upon his fatherless children.
Let his posterity be destroyed,
  and in the next generation let their name be clean put out (Ps. cix. 12, 13).

I WAS speaking last Sunday about the narrative in the 15th chapter of the first book of Samuel, and the command laid upon Saul to exterminate Amalek; and pointed out how such a command, though it might by various considerations be to some degree palliated or explained (as belonging to an immature and imperfect dispensation), could not, if judged by the standard which Christ has taught us, be regarded otherwise than inhuman and unjust. I propose this morning to continue the same subject; to consider some other instances in which the spirit of the older dispensation is not the spirit of

Christ, and to offer some considerations in explanation of the fact.

The Psalm from which I have taken my text is one of those which are commonly known as the Imprecatory Psalms—Psalms in which the poet utters impassioned prayers for vengeance on his enemies, and dwells with manifest satisfaction on one aspect after another of their expected doom. The two Psalms in which this feeling comes out most thoroughly are the 69th and the 109th: but there are others in which it is also present. For instance, 'the righteous shall rejoice, when he seeth the vengeance. He shall wash his feet in the blood of the ungodly.' The Psalmist in each case is in distress, and need, and prays earnestly for deliverance out of it; but the tone of the two Psalms is substantially the same: so it will be sufficient if we confine ourselves to the 109th. The Psalmist here cries to God for help; he complains that certain malignant foes—we cannot say definitely who they are—have, without any provocation on his part, brought against him false and malicious charges: 'They have rewarded me evil for good, and hatred for my good will.' Then he singles out, as it seems, the ringleader, and utters upon him a series of anathemas, imprecating upon him and his family misfortune and trouble in every department of life. 'Set thou a wicked man over him, and let an accuser stand at his right hand.' Let him, i.e. when arraigned in a court of justice, have no chance of acquittal, let him have not only an unjust judge, but a malicious accuser to bring about his ruin: 'when sentence is given upon him let him be condemned, and let his prayer be turned into sin,' i.e. may his prayer to God for mercy have the very opposite effect, and draw down upon him the divine wrath. May his life come to a speedy termination, and leave his position vacant for another. 'Let his days be few, and let another take his office.' May his family and children suffer with him: 'Let his children be vagabonds and beg their bread; let them seek it also out of their desolate places,' i.e. out of their ruined homes. 'Let there be no man to pity him, nor to have compassion upon his fatherless children. Let his posterity be cut off and in the next generation let their name be clean put out.' And he ends by the wish that trouble and misfortune may be his constant, inseparable attendant through the years which yet remain to him. ' Let it be unto him as the cloke that he putteth on, and as the girdle that he is alway girded withal. Let it thus happen for the Lord unto mine enemies, and to those that speak evil against my soul.' And then the Psalmist closes by repeating his prayer for deliverance out of his need.

The verses which I have taken for my text are explicable in themselves by the principle I referred to last Sunday. The ancients did not distinguish, as we do, the individual man ; they regarded him as forming a whole with his family, or (it might be) his nation : a criminal's family was often punished with him ; and so it seemed to the Psalmist perfectly natural, and in entire accord with his manner of thinking, to wish that a man's kith and kin should be implicated in his doom.

But there remains the further and wider question : **How comes it that we find the**

CIX]   THE PSALMS

lofty and spiritual meditations which undoubtedly constitute the greater part of the Psalms interrupted at times by passages which strike such a different and discordant note ? How can the men who wrote them be regarded as in any sense inspired by the Holy Spirit ?

Various explanations have been suggested— some so forced and unnatural that they are not worth alluding to ; and others merely of a partial character, accounting only for some of the passages, and leaving the others unexplained. One is, for example, to explain the imprecations away by rendering the verbs as *futures*, and regarding them merely as *declarations* of the certain fate of the wicked. But though this might be possible in some cases, there are others in which grammar does not permit such a rendering ; so that this explanation does not remove the difficulty.

We evidently need an explanation which is wider and more comprehensive, and, in seeking for it, we must remember that these psalms do not stand alone. There are similar passages, for instance, in Jeremiah. The prophet Jeremiah was unpopular, and met with persecution on account of his predictions of disaster : on one occasion the people of his own native place sought his life ; in other ways also he suffered for righteousness' sake, very much as was the case with many of the Psalmists. And so speaking of his enemies, he says in his 11th chapter, ' O Lord of hosts that judgest righteously, let me see Thy vengeance on them : for unto Thee I have revealed my cause.' And again, in the 15th chapter, ' O Lord, Thou knowest : remember and visit me, and avenge me of my persecutors,' and in the 17th chapter, ' Let them be ashamed that persecute me, but let not me be ashamed ; let them be dismayed, but let not me be dismayed : bring upon them the day of evil, and destroy them with a double destruction.' And even more strongly, in his 18th chapter, in language very much like that of Psalm cix., ' Shall evil be recompensed for good ? for they have digged a pit for my soul. Remember how I stood before Thee to speak good for them, to turn away Thy fury from them.' But like the Psalmist he cannot bear that his good will should be met

CIX]   THE PSALMS

by evil, and so he prays, 'Therefore deliver
Thou up their children to the famine, and
give them over to the power of the sword;
let their wives become childless and widows;
let their men be slain of death, and their young
men smitten of the sword in battle. Thou
knowest, Lord, all their counsel against me
to slay me : forgive not their iniquity, neither
blot out their sin from Thy sight ; let them
be overthrown before Thee ; deal Thou with
them in the time of Thine anger.' These
are the feelings of an individual : elsewhere
we find national feeling expressing itself in
a similar strain. The men of Judah suffered
severely at the hands of the Chaldaeans, and
also of their neighbours the Edomites : by
the former their city had been captured,
sacked and burnt, and they themselves carried
into captivity ; while the Edomites stood by
and manifested open and malicious exultation
at the disaster thus overtaking Jerusalem.
Some time afterwards, probably two generations, two prophets arose to declare the doom
imminent on the Chaldaeans and on Edom
—the authors of the prophecies which now

form the 34th chapter of Isaiah and of Jeremiah l.–li. ; but, not content with simply announcing as a fact the doom of the two nations, they dwell with evident delight on the prospect of their fall, and on the details of ruin which will accompany it ; a glow of passion animates their works : they breathe of vengeance and satisfaction at the impending catastrophe. And one writer, a Psalmist, the author of a Psalm which is in some respects one of the most beautiful and pathetic Psalms in the Psalter, can bring himself to utter the terrible felicitation, instinct with the barbarism of the most savage warfare : ' Happy shall he be that taketh thy children, and dasheth them against the stones ! '

And so even the Evangelical prophet, the author of Isaiah xl.–lx., pictures the Divine conqueror returning from Edom, after a great slaughter there, his garments crimson, and his feet streaming with Idumaean blood.

The utterances of which I have given examples may be excused, or palliated, but it is idle to pretend that they breathe the spirit of Christ, or could be appropriated consistently by His followers. It is true, no doubt, for instance, that they are in a sense 'the feeling after a truth of the divine government of the world.' The Prophets and Psalmists had a keen sense of the great conflict constantly going on between good and evil, between God and His enemies. In the world at large this conflict was waged between Israel as the people of God, and the nations which threatened to destroy Israel. The enemies of Israel were the enemies of Israel's God : Israel's defeat was a reproach to His name : the cause at stake was not merely the existence of the nation, but the cause of divine truth and righteousness as well. Within the nation of Israel the same conflict was also being waged on a smaller scale between the godly and the ungodly. When the righteous were oppressed, and the wicked triumphant, it seemed as though God's rule were being set at nought, as though His cause were losing. It was not only allowable, but a duty, to pray for its triumph ; and that involved the destruction of the wicked, who perished in their wickedness. The prophet who wished the enemies of his nation destroyed, the Psalmist who desired to see the downfall of his own enemies, or the enemies of the godly party to which he belonged and with which he identified himself, was thus really desirous of advancing the cause of righteousness, and the establishment of God's kingdom : he was actuated at bottom by a holy and righteous zeal. Moreover, the ancient Israelites had no revelation—or at least no distinct revelation—of a future and final judgement upon all men : they expected and desired to see a present and visible distinction between the righteous and the wicked. But God's sentence upon evil is in many cases deferred and not immediately visible ; hence there was the greater eagerness to see it executed promptly and immediately ; and the righteous could rejoice when he saw this take place, for it was a manifest proof of the righteous government of Jehovah. There underlay the utterances we have been considering a real and justifiable zeal for truth and right.

These considerations, as I have said, may palliate the difficulty ; but they do not remove

CIX] THE PSALMS

it altogether. There is a personal element, an element of personal feeling and vindictiveness, which remains, and which cannot be eliminated. The foes of the Psalmist, or of Jeremiah, may have been hostile to a *cause*, but they have also attacked and persecuted a *person*; and the personal feeling thus aroused is what finds expression in the imprecations which have been quoted. And it is just this feeling of personal hate and personal animosity which, judged by the standpoint of Christian ethics, stands condemned. We must admit it; and can only see in it the voice of persecuted righteousness not yet freed from discord by the precept and example of Christ. The religion of Israel taught the people many high moral duties—not only those involved in the Ten Commandments—forbidding, for example, hatred, vengeance, and bearing of grudges, at least towards members of their own nation: it taught them in various ways to educate their affections, and to discipline their passions; but there were particular points at which this discipline, judged by the highest standard, was not perfect. The occurrence in the Old Testament of passages expressing this imperfect spirit, will occasion difficulty only through a crude and mechanical view of inspiration. Without to-day inquiring what is involved in inspiration, it is certain that there is in the Bible a human element as well as a divine element : it is manifest, for example, even in the different styles in which different Biblical writers express themselves ; and we have no right to assume without inquiry that it is limited to literary characteristics. The inspiration of the Biblical writers conferred upon them a rare and unique spiritual insight ; but it did not suppress their individuality and independence ; nor have we any antecedent right to suppose that every writer is subordinated to its influence in precisely the same degree. We cannot come to the Bible with a theory of inspiration, we must frame our theory of inspiration *from* the Bible ; and it must be such as will explain the facts which the Bible contains. We must not have a theory which will imply that God is the immediate author of a vindictive temper in His ser-

THE PSALMS

vants. Neither Scripture nor the judgement of the Church authorises us to affirm that every statement rests upon the same moral or religious plane, or is in the same measure the expression of the divine mind; and the passages I have been considering to-day must be regarded as passages in which the voice of God is not heard with the clearness and directness which is usual in Scripture. The Psalmists do largely express their own personal experiences and feelings; and their feelings and thoughts possess unquestionably, as a rule, the highest spirituality; but there are instances in which the case is different; and in these we are obliged to suppose that they have not been completely subordinated to the spirit of God, and that the voice of human passion is heard in them, in a manner which is intelligible, perhaps even justifiable, in the age in which the authors wrote, but which is not in harmony with the higher moral level on which Christ has placed us. The Old Testament contains a progressive revelation; and it is the essence of what progresses, that the earlier stages should be less perfect and less mature than those which come after. And so, in spite of the fact that there are many points, including the more important ones—such as the broader duties towards God and one's neighbour—in which the spirit of the Old Testament is not substantially different from that of the New Testament, there are others in which the case is different, and the subject I have been considering to-day is one of them. The difference between the two dispensations was well exemplified by the two Morning Lessons on St. James' day, which fell during the past week. One is a narrative in the Book of Kings. Elijah had once called down fire from heaven to destroy the soldiers who came to take him. This was the first Lesson. In the second Lesson we heard the rebuke addressed by Christ to the two disciples who, appealing to this narrative, desired Him in like manner to call down fire upon the village which had refused to receive Him : ' Ye know not what manner of spirit ye are of '—ye know not by what manner of spirit, as followers of Christ, ye ought to be actuated, the spirit of

CIX] THE PSALMS

love, not of sternness, of gentleness, not of vengeance. The spirit of vengeance and retaliation, the spirit of hatred and persecution, the spirit of uncharitableness, is one which is with difficulty eradicated from human nature ; and instances could be quoted in which Christian writers and even Christian teachers have given expression to it. In the middle ages it is said to have been a custom to hire monks for the purpose of reciting the 109th Psalm as a curse against an enemy. Such things have passed away now ; but there are corners of the human heart in which the same spirit still sometimes lurks, and out of which it sometimes breaks on unexpected occasions. There is still need that we should repeat with earnestness the prayer in the Litany, 'From envy, hatred, and malice and all uncharitableness, Good Lord deliver us.'

PSALM VIII

PSALM VIII

When I consider Thy heavens, the work of Thy fingers
the moon and the stars, which Thou hast ordained ⁺
What is man that Thou art mindful of him ?
and the Son of man, that Thou visitest him ?
For Thou hast made him but little lower than God,
and crownest him with glory and state (Ps. viii. 3 f.).

MAN, how small and yet how great, is the thought which, with singular poetic skill, is set forth in this familiar Psalm. Who the poet is to whose words we are listening we do not indeed know : for though the title assigns the Psalm to David, the titles of the Psalms are, in many cases, so manifestly contradicted by the contents that it is clear they cannot have been appended by the author himself, and it is doubtful whether they even embody a genuine tradition ; and the 8th Psalm seems to reflect a maturer stage of thought, a deeper vein of meditation, than is likely to have been attained in the early age of David.

To understand a Psalm, however, and take home the lesson which it brings, it is not necessary to know who wrote it ; its value is dependent not upon its being the work of a particular author, but upon its contents ; it is sufficient to study it in itself ; to consider its purpose and object, and the thoughts of which it is the expression.

The 8th Psalm is the first of a number of Psalms which celebrate the praise of God in the phenomena of the natural world. The sun by day in the 19th Psalm, the moon and the stars by night in this Psalm, the thunderstorm—more impressive often in Palestine than with us—in the 29th Psalm, the harvest, as evidencing God's care for his creatures, in the 65th Psalm, the glory and order of Creation in the 104th Psalm, are all dwelt upon by the Hebrew poets, and described with a force, animation, a wealth of imaginative colouring, which have never been surpassed. But the Hebrew odes are never merely descriptive. Nature is never regarded

VIII] THE PSALMS

in them as an end in herself. She is an instrument in the hand of God, the means by which He manifests His powers. The sense of God's presence, of which the Psalmists are so profoundly conscious in their own spiritual life, is that which gives its glory and its meaning to the natural world. Their vivid realization of God's presence, as of a presence which fills the world, and from which there is no escape, is impressed upon their poetry of nature. Nature is instinct with the marks and evidences of His glory. The sun and the moon are His witnesses and heralds, the light is His robe, the storm-cloud is His chariot, within which He rides shrouded in light, the thunder is His voice, the lightning flashes are the partings of the cloud revealing glimpses of the brilliancy shining within. Admiration of nature is a confession of the glory and power of God which are stamped upon it.

O Jehovah, our Lord,
How glorious is Thy Name in all the earth,
Thou that hast set Thy majesty upon the heavens.

The Psalmist looks out upon the physical

world, and sees in it the reflection of the nature and character of God. The 'Name' of God means as often in The Old Testament the *nature* of God, as revealed or made manifest to man, i.e. here the expression of Himself in the works of creation and providence by which His hand or character may be discerned. The Psalmist does not say, How *excellent* is Thy name in all the earth; he says, How *noble* or *glorious* it is: the Divine nature is manifest in the earth in grandeur: it shines forth in glory and greatness to the eye of faith from the works of nature. Jehovah has, moreover, set His majesty also upon the heavens. He has clothed them with a royal splendour—such is the sense of the original expression—which is a reflexion and manifestation of his own.

Out of the mouths of babes and sucklings hast thou founded strength,
Because of thine adversaries,
To still the enemy and the avenger.

Even the feeblest representatives of humanity may be God's champions to confound and silence those who oppose His kingdom and deny His goodness and providential government. The enemy and the avenger (or rather the self-avenger, the vengeful man) are those who oppose God's purposes or question His providence, and those who usurp, in their own selfish interests, a judicial function which belongs to God alone. The thought is already in the Psalmist's mind which afterwards comes out more distinctly—the contrast between Jehovah, with whose glory the earth is filled, and who has arrayed the heavens in His majesty, and has yet, paradoxical as it may appear, conferred powers and capacities upon man, to which his puny material structure might have seemed unequal. Thus by 'babes and sucklings' he means doubtless men such as himself, feeble and imperfect representatives of human nature, who nevertheless may become instruments in God's hand able to put to shame the scornful or defiant adversary.

The Psalmist passes now to a different thought:

When I consider Thy heavens, the work of Thy fingers,
The moon and the stars which Thou hast ordained.
What is man that Thou art mindful of him?
The Son of man that Thou visitest him?

The contemplation of the heavens in all their splendour[1] forces the Psalmist to wonder that God could choose so insignificant a being as man for the object of His special regard. It is manifestly of the sky by night that the Psalmist is thinking : for he does not mention the sun ; and the star-lit sky, especially as seen through the transparent clearness of the Eastern atmosphere, is obviously much more impressive, much more suggestive of the vastness and variety of the universe, than the sky as visible by day. The vault of heaven, forming, as it seems to do, a vast canopy overhanging the earth, the stars appearing infinite in number, each keeping its appointed place, our own brilliant satellite, month by month fulfilling its course, each and all seeming to belong to a higher and wider order of things than anything upon earth, while man is powerless to raise himself above the ground he treads on—all this makes the thoughtful spectator feel how small a portion of the universe he is, how little he must be in the eyes of the Intelli-

---

[1] With this paragraph comp. a passage from Whewell's *Astronomy*, cited by Perowne, *ad loc.*

gence which can embrace the whole. And if this be the feeling aroused even in the untaught mind, how infinitely must the impression be deepened in one who looks on the universe in the light of modern astronomy, and who can realize the distances and the magnitudes, and the finely regulated movements, of the vast system of stars visible in the heavens, to a degree of which the ancient Hebrew Psalmist had no conception; and who can also form at least an imperfect idea of the incalculable ages which have been occupied with the process of making them what they now are. But in spite of the vastness of the interval which here separates him from those majestic works of creation, man, mortal, frail, earth-born, is the object of God's regard: He is both mindful of him, and visits him: he is not lost to His omniscience; and His ' visitation ' —that is, His constant and continuous providential regard—sustains his life, supplies his needs, and ministers to his happiness.

Thou hast made him but little lower than God;
Thou crownest him with glory and state:
Thou makest him to rule over the works of Thy hands;

Thou hast put all things under his feet.
All sheep and oxen,
Yea, and the beasts of the field,
The fowl of the air and the fish of the sea,
Whatsoever passeth through the paths of the sea.

The Psalmist looks back upon man's creation. God's regard was further shown in the nature with which man was then endowed, and the position of sovereignty in which he was placed. He was made to be but little lower than God, or to lack but little of being God. The reference no doubt is to what is termed in Genesis i. man's creation 'in the image of God,' by which is meant his possession of *self-conscious reason*—an adumbration, we may suppose, however faint, of the supreme mind of God—the faculty separating man from the brute creation, enabling him to *know* in a sense in which the animals do not know, to act with deliberate forethought and adaptation of means to ends, to originate—a power which may be said to correspond in some measure, though of course in an infinitely lower degree, with the creative will of God, the faculty in virtue of which he is capable of articulate speech, which is the expression of the rational mind, and has the capacity of distinguishing not only, as the animals do, pleasure and pain, but also right and wrong, and the power to a certain degree of apprehending God, and of holding communion with Him. These faculties of knowledge, thought, speech, discovery, origination, invention—this power of apprehending religious and moral truth, these intellectual and spiritual endowments, which raise man above sense and time and merely material considerations, which elevate him above the brutes and ally him with God, and which are all dependent on, and are, in fact, parts of the one supreme and princely gift of self-conscious reason, are what is meant when it is said that man is created 'in the image of God'; and they are what are alluded to here when the Psalmist describes him as made 'but a little lower than God.' He is crowned further with glory and state, the attributes of royalty; he is crowned, as we might say, king of creation. He is made to rule over the works of God's creative hand: all things are put under his feet, as it is said in the Book of Genesis, 'and let them have dominion over the fish of the sea, and over the fowl of the air, and over the cattle, and over all the earth and over every creeping thing that creepeth upon the earth.' The earth in all its parts is subject to man's sway. And so man's subjects are as it were mustered and passed in review by the poet : domestic animals, the wild creatures that roam at large over the open country, the fish of the sea, and all other denizens of the ocean-depths. In our day it would be by the discovery of the laws and processes of nature, and the utilisation of the great forces and material agents supplied by nature—steam, water, light, electricity, for instance—that man's sovereignty would be most strikingly illustrated : in the Psalmist's day, in the free, outdoor life of the East, it would be most conspicuously displayed in his mastery over the animal creation, which he tamed, or caught, and turned variously to his own use. And the poet ends as he began, with the same exclamation of reverent wonder :—

O Jehovah, our Lord, how glorious is Thy name in all
    the earth.

VIII] THE PSALMS

The sovereignty of God is revealed both in His own rule over nature, and also in the delegated authority which man, as it were His viceroy upon earth, exercises over it.

Man, then, not nature; man, how small in comparison with the starry heavens, how great in view of the powers with which he is endowed, and the sovereignty conferred upon him, is the central thought in the poet's mind. The dignity of human nature, man's material insignificance, and yet at the same time the continual care lavished upon him by the Creator, and the kingly prerogative of reason, with all that this involves, wherewith he has endowed him, is the theme of the Psalm. Insignificant as he is in comparison with the stately magnificence of nature—he is in truth more wonderful and mysterious than they, and he is by nature scarce less than Divine, and appointed to be God's viceroy in the world.

The Psalm should lead us to reflect on the respect with which human nature should be treated even in the person of its humblest representatives, and on the ultimate destiny involved in the prerogatives thus conferred upon it, if it does not wilfully renounce it, viz., the blessedness of communion and life with God hereafter. It should also lead us to remember the responsibilities which the possession of a faculty such as reason imposes on us: the moral limitations by which its unbounded exercise should be restrained, the manner in which it should be used to rule and regulate the passions, and its employment in order to subordinate sordid or selfish ambitions and aims to those which, in one way or another, ennoble or elevate or benefit mankind.

The Psalmist looks away from the Fall, from the sin and failure and rebellion of mankind, to man's nature and position and destiny in the original purpose of God. The image of God in man is defaced but not destroyed, and he still retains dominion over the earth. But in the absoluteness—the universality—of the terms used, the Psalm contemplates man in his ideal nature: it is only to man in the ultimate goal and scope of

VIII]   THE PSALMS

his destiny that all things are subjected. And so the author of the Epistle to the Hebrews in the 2nd chapter quotes the Psalm, and, urging that the words ' Thou hast put all things under his feet ' can have not yet been literally fulfilled in man, declares that their proper fulfilment is only to be seen in Jesus, Whom God had made a little lower than the angels and crowned with glory and state. It is not quoted as a prophecy of Christ; it is quoted as showing that man's destiny, as reported in the Psalm, finds its true and fullest accomplishment only in the Son of man, in the ideal representative of the human race, whose power extends literally over all creation. The true destiny of man, as described by the Psalm, has been missed by man himself: the actual condition of things falls short of it; it is fulfilled in another sense than had been expected, by Him Who, being more than man, took man's nature upon Him, and became thereby the perfect representative of humanity. And so the Psalm is used as one of the special Psalms for Ascension Day; for it is in the Ascension, the final triumph of

Christ's life on earth, that we see man, in the person of his ideal representative, crowned most conspicuously with 'glory and state.'

PSALM XV

PSALM XV

Lord, who shall dwell in thy tabernacle :
   or who shall rest upon thy holy hill ?
Even he that leadeth an uncorrupt life :
   and doeth the thing which is right, and speak-
      the truth from his heart.
He that hath used no deceit in his tongue, nor
      done evil to his neighbour :
   and hath not slandered his neighbour.
He that setteth not by himself, but is lowly in
      his own eyes :
   and maketh much of them that fear the Lord.
He that sweareth unto his neighbour and dis-
      appointeth him not :
   though it were to his own hindrance.
He that hath not given his money upon usury :
   nor taken reward against the innocent.
Whoso doeth these things :
   shall never fall.

THE subject of our reflections this evening is to be *goodness*. The term is a comprehensive one, and at first sight it may seem to include several of the other graces which are named by the Apostle as the fruit of the Spirit. But if we notice them carefully, we shall observe that the others are either states of the soul itself, as *joy* and *peace*, or else they are the qualities which would show themselves in special circumstances, or towards particular persons, as *long-suffering* under provocation, or *kindness* towards those who were in a position to receive it. *Goodness*, however, is rather the quality which would determine the character generally, and guide a person in his actions in the ordinary and usual circumstances of everyday life, without reference to any special and exceptional occasions which might demand the exercise of special corresponding graces. And it seemed to me difficult to find a more suggestive and winning picture of goodness, exhibited not in the abstract, but in a concrete character, than is afforded by the short but beautiful Psalm which I have just read.

Such is the picture of an ideal character, drawn by the pen of some ancient Hebrew Psalmist. It is an anticipation of the quality of goodness, enumerated by the Apostle among

XV] THE PSALMS

the graces of the Spirit. It is attractively drawn : and the language, while its general sense is sufficiently plain, nevertheless either expresses or suggests more than is apparent at first sight.

> Lord, who shall sojourn in Thy tabernacle ?
> who shall dwell in Thy holy hill ?

Who is worthy to be a citizen of Zion ? Such is the question which the short and well-known Psalm, of which I have quoted the opening words, supplies the answer. Who is worthy to dwell in the immediate presence of Jehovah, to enjoy His protection and blessing ? The Psalmist asks his question figuratively : ' Lord, who shall sojourn in Thy tent, and who shall dwell in Thy holy hill ? The word *sojourn* means here, *stay as a guest*. Hospitality in the Eastern countries is a virtue that is highly esteemed ; and a traveller who comes on his journey to the tent of an Arab will be entertained by him, and while he is with him will be sure, even though he be a stranger, of his host's protection and friendship. It is from this custom that the Psalmist borrows his figure; he means to say, who will have the right to sojourn as a guest in Jehovah's tent, and enjoy the protection and friendship which his acceptance there would afford him? In the next line he uses a rather stronger term: who shall *dwell* upon Thy holy hill, i.e., who shall be accepted, not as a passing guest only, but as a permanent dweller on God's holy hill? Dwelling on God's holy hill is a figure derived from the custom of resorting to the Temple, the spot chosen by God for His abode upon earth, for worship, and meaning to enjoy the privilege of being constantly near to God, or holding communion with Him. Who, he asks, will enjoy God's protection, and the privilege of constant access to Him? In what follows the character of the man to whom God will grant these privileges is drawn out in detail.

The Psalmist first describes it in general terms, he then illustrates it by certain special examples, showing the manner in which such a

He that walketh perfectly, and worketh righteousness,
    and speaketh truth with his heart.

person would act in cases likely to arise. He whose life, viewed as a whole, is free from flaw or blemish ; who is whole-hearted towards God, and sincere and without reproach in his dealings with men.

Consistency is a virtue the importance of which some people are apt to forget. They do what is right so long as it serves their purpose, or is required by their respectability ; but when occasion offers, or they no longer dread the consequences of a discovery, they are heedless what they do, and fall into evil. The man who walks perfectly, the consistent man, is one who sets before himself a right and good ideal, and endeavours conscientiously to act up to it, not deviating from it when temptation offers, but adhering to it steadily. He who *walketh* in righteousness, i.e. one who is ever striving to show and exhibit his righteousness in action : a succession of *acts* of righteousness are to mark his dealings with his relations, his friends, his neighbours, and all others with whom he is brought into contact. This evidently opens for him a wide sphere of duty : he is to *do* righteousness on all the opportunities which his daily life affords him of doing it; it is to be his rule, alike in his business and in his pleasure, in whatever he sets his hand to.

'And speaketh truth with his heart.' The truth which he speaks with his lips has its source in his heart: it is not a labour with him to frame his lips to utter it; it springs up spontaneously from within him, and hence he is said to speak it *with his heart*. His conduct and acts have been spoken of already; and here the Psalmist comes to speak of his words. Truth is at home in his heart, and hence his mouth speaks it naturally and as a matter of course: it never occurs to him to utter anything different from it, anything which is at variance with the truth as he knows it in his heart. Truthfulness is a virtue which can never be too highly prized: it is one of the bonds which hold society together, and make common life, and common action, and combination for common ends, possible. Let us accustom ourselves, then, to *think* the truth; if we do that the words which we speak will correspond with it as a matter of course : we shall *speak the truth with our heart*.

Hitherto, the Psalmist has described what the man with whom God will hold communion *does* do : he now passes on to mention some of the things which he does *not* do.

> He that slandereth not with his tongue,
>   nor doeth evil to his friend,
>   nor taketh up a reproach against his neighbour.

He is one who is careful never to injure others either by word or deed—he slanders not with his tongue, nor does evil to a friend or companion, one who is associated with him in any business or enterprise ; and thirdly, he never takes up a reproach against his neighbour, i.e., he neither starts a false report concerning him, nor, if one reaches him, does he propagate it further. The cases instanced are typical examples of our duty towards our neighbour, and they are examples of duties which the temptation is often very strong to neglect. The man who can style himself God's guest will be free from every touch of malice. He will not spread an ill-natured report concerning a neighbour. If a tale of scandal reaches his ears, he will not repeat it. He will not put forth vague imputations against another, with the view of damaging his credit, or bringing him into disrepute among his neighbours or acquaintance. He will bring into prominence the good qualities in a person's character. If there are any deficiencies, occasions of course may arise in which it will be his duty to speak of them, but he will not do so unnecessarily, nor will he find a pleasure in so doing. If he is engaged in some common undertaking with others, he will not seek to obtain some unfair advantage over them ; nor will he seek by dishonest or underhand means to injure his fellows. In one word, he will be guided by the precept, ' Thou shalt love thy neighbour as thyself.'

> In whose eyes a reprobate is contemned ;
> > but he honoureth them that fear the Lord :
> > he that sweareth to his own hurt, and changeth not.

He is one, i.e., who turns away from the evil and honours the good, and who regards the sanctity of an oath as inviolable. He will not associate with persons who are reprobate, and deserve to be rejected, because they will only corrupt and infect the character of those who consort with them; the wealth or reputation or popularity which they may possess will have no attractions for him. On the contrary, he will *honour* those who are worthy of honour—the true worshippers and servants of God, who live consistent lives, and whose example and companionship is a help and gain to those who are brought into contact with them. The sense of the last line of this verse is paraphrased or given more fully in the P. B. V.: 'He that sweareth to his neighbour and disappointeth him not, though it be to his own hindrance.' The sanctity of an oath, or of a solemn promise generally, is what the Psalmist has in mind. If a man has made an engagement to do something for another, and finds that it involves some unforeseen disadvantage to himself, he does not alter the terms of his promise so as to make them more favourable to himself, but adheres to them. He shows truthfulness in *act*, just as before he was said to show truthfulness in *word*. It is the principle which is at the root of what we term *honesty*, especially in connexion with trade. A man, for example, who purports to supply a good article, and passes off an inferior one in its place, has really *changed* what he promised to give his customer, for the sake of receiving additional gain for himself. And thus he has offended against the spirit, if not against the letter, of the Psalmist's words.

The last verse is:

> He that putteth not out his money to usury,
> nor taketh reward against the innocent.

By 'usury' here is meant what we should now term *interest*. This characteristic of the God-fearing man may strike us, perhaps, at first, as somewhat strange : many excellent Christians invest their money in different ways, and receive interest for it ; can it be that they are really acting counter to what the Psalmist deemed to be right ? No : and the reason is this ; the Psalmist, by 'usury' or 'interest', meant something that was really different from what we should denote by those terms. In ancient times, the practice of lending money on interest was connected with very grave abuses, from which, in modern times, at least if carried on by honourable persons, it is free: and on account of these abuses the practice was condemned, not by the Psalmist only, but by ancient writers generally—in ancient Greece as well as among the Israelites. In modern times, the chief purpose for which money is borrowed is to conduct some great commercial undertaking, which a single person has not the means to carry on himself, and therefore is obliged to obtain a loan from others; and it is just as reasonable that persons who lend money to such a concern should receive some return for their loan, i.e., as we say, *interest* for it, as that they should receive a return for any other loan that they make—for instance, a loan of a house, or furniture, or other goods. But in ancient times money was not usually borrowed for such purposes as these: it was borrowed by needy persons to save themselves from ruin; and if they could not repay it, they and their families were liable to become the slaves of the creditor. There is an instance of this in 2 Kings iv. 1, where a widow comes to Elisha to seek his help, on the ground that her husband is dead, and that the 'creditor is come to take away her two children to be bondmen' (or 'slaves'). As this was too often the result of money-lending in ancient days, the practice was viewed with great disfavour ; and the habit of receiving interest for money was regarded as taking advantage of a person in his need; it was associated with everything that was selfish and grasping and hard-hearted and cruel. Hence the man who is worthy to be the guest of God does not 'put out his money upon usury,' i.e. does not put it out in the manner and for the purposes which were usual in ancient times, when this Psalm was written. But the Psalmist does not condemn the lending of money by honourable men for legitimate purposes of trade, in which the borrower may often be benefited even more than the lender. What he does condemn is the grasping and selfish spirit which takes an unfair and dishonest advantage of a neighbour's need, and which, in his days was associated with the xv] THE PSALMS

lending of money. And it is, of course, true that there are persons now, those commonly called 'money-lenders,' who are only too apt to take dishonest advantage of those who borrow of them, who extort from them exorbitant interest, and drag them more and more into their power. And, naturally, practices such as these would not be regarded by the Psalmist as compatible with his ideal of a true servant of God.

'Nor taketh reward against the innocent,' i.e. takes a bribe, whether as judge or witness, to bring about the condemnation of an innocent person. In Eastern countries justice is seldom administered purely; and accordingly the Old Testament inculcates, with great earnestness and frequency, purity of judgment, and abounds with denunciations against those who administer it corruptly. This is a fault from which a modern Christian country, such as our own, is no doubt practically free: we can hardly imagine the case of a judge accepting a bribe; and though witnesses may occasionally be bribed to secure the acquittal of an offender, it surely can never happen that they are bribed to condemn a person who is innocent. But if we refer the special case taken by the Psalmist to the principle which underlies it, we shall see that it is the quality of fairness, equity, integrity, coupled with a considerate regard for the claims and rights of those who may, in some way or other, be placed in our power. The man whom God will admit to His friendship and protection is one who is fair and just and equitable, and will never lower himself to any unjust or dishonourable transaction, nor seek to oppress, or take an unjust advantage of, one who is in any way dependent upon him.

'He that doeth these things shall never be moved.'

Such a man may not take up his dwelling in the earthly courts of God; but, at least, he will enjoy, under His protection, unshaken prosperity. Integrity of life is a man's confidence, and unfailing source of strength. The man who adheres to it will never make a false step or find himself in a false position. 'He that doeth these things shall never be moved.' Such is the portrait of a blameless life drawn by the pen of a Jewish poet. It is difficult to imagine one purer or brighter. It shows us what we so often have need to be recalled to us, that a genuine faith in God cannot be severed from integrity of life : that religion is no excuse for a lax morality, that true love of God is the life and bond of any social virtue. Each line gives us a standard which we may apply to ourselves. To speak truth with our heart, to spread no slander against a neighbour, to be blameless in word and deed, to take no bribe against the innocent, to treat no one with hardness and injustice, are not these typical examples of the principles which cover the greater part of our duty towards our neighbour, and will they not guide us rightly through most of the daily course and business of life ? Let us keep this ideal before our eyes ; and endeavour, by God's grace, to realize it as far as possible in ourselves.

PSALM LXXII

PSALM LXXII

> Give the king Thy judgements, O God,
> and Thy righteousness unto the king's son.
> —Psalm lxxii. 1.

THESE familiar words form the opening verse of a Psalm which depicts the ideal of a godly king. Who the king was with regard to whom the words were spoken, we do not know : it was pretty clearly one of the later kings—possibly Josiah. The Psalm reads as though it were written at the time of the king's accession ; and the poet prays that God will confer upon him the gifts that will enable him to fulfil the ideal of his office, and to prove himself a beneficent and righteous ruler.

> Give the king Thy judgements, O God,
> and Thy righteousness unto the king's son.

May God give the king a store of His judgements, or decisions, that he may appropriate and apply them, when cases come before him for judgement; and may He endow him, as the son of a royal father, with a divine sense of justice that may make him a worthy ruler. May he, the poet continues, judge God's people with righteousness, and his poor—these common victims of oppression and injustice under an Oriental government —with judgement; may peace and righteousness flourish in his land; may his rule be as gentle and beneficent as the rain coming down upon the mown grass, and as drops that water the earth!

Next, taking a bolder flight, the poet prays that his realm may be wider than Solomon's, that all enemies may be subdued before him and that the most distant and famous peoples may do him homage—'May he have dominion also from sea to sea, and from the Euphrates to the ends of the earth! May the desert dwellers'—the wild Bedawin, the free sons of the desert, who will not readily own any superior—'may the desert dwellers bow before him, and his enemies lick the dust! May the kings of Tarshish and of the isles'—of Tartessus in distant Spain, and the isles and coasts of the Mediterranean Sea—'render presents, May the kings of Sheba'—in South Arabia— 'and Seba'—in Abyssinia—'bring dues! Yea, may all kings fall down before him, may all nations do him service!'

The vision of a world-wide dominion, and of a world-wide homage, rises here in the poet's mind; but the king's claim to it rests upon the justice and mercifulness of his rule. As before, his special merit is his care for the poor and the oppressed—

> For he will deliver the needy when he crieth,
>   the poor also, and him that hath no helper.
> He will have pity on the feeble and the needy,
>   and the lives of the needy He will save;
> He will redeem their souls from oppression and wrong,
>   and precious will their blood be in His sight.

And the Psalmist closes with three final prayers for the welfare of the king, the prosperity of his land and people, and the honourable perpetuation of his name. 'So may he live! and may there be given unto him of the gold of Sheba! May prayer also be made for him'—not, as in the Prayer Book Version, '*to* him'—'continually! and daily may he be blessed! May there be abundance of corn in the land upon the top of the mountains; may the fruit thereof shake like Lebanon: and may men blossom out of the city like the herbage of the earth! May his name endure for ever! May his name be perpetuated'— by his descendants—'as long as the sun endureth! May men also bless themselves by him'—i.e. use his name in blessing as a type of happiness, saying, God make thee like this king!—'May all nations call him happy'!

Such are the prayers and splendid anticipations which on a gala day were expressed by some poet of Israel on behalf of a newly anointed king of his people. The poet's thoughts move along lines suggested partly by reminiscences of the happy reign of Solomon, partly by a sense of what the qualifications of a just ruler should be, under the social conditions of the time. But the poet, in the hopes and anticipations which he puts forth, includes more than could be realized by any actual king of Israel, and portrays in fact an *ideal* king, whose just and perfect rule extends to the ends of the earth, and commands the homage of the world. And in so far as he does this, he looks out beyond the actual king whose accession he celebrates, and constructs a picture of the ideal king of Israel, whom we call the Messiah.

But it is not on this aspect of the Psalm that I desire to dwell further to-day. The blessings of a wise and beneficent rule are often alluded to in the Old Testament. In a poem in the 2nd Book of Samuel called the 'Last words of David' the blessings of such a rule are compared beautifully to the life-giving sunshine of a cloudless morning, when after rain the earth appears clad with fresh young verdure—

> When one ruleth over men righteously,
> > ruleth in the fear of God,
> then is it as the light of the morning when the sun
> > ariseth,
> > a morning without clouds,
> > when through clear shining after rain,
> > the young grass springeth out of the earth.

And the ideal king is depicted in the prophets

as doing, like David and Solomon, judgement and justice in the land, as defending the cause of the poor, and delivering him from oppression and wrong, as punishing the wrong-doer, and by a wise and just rule maintaining the prosperity of his people. In the 101st Psalm we have what has been called a 'mirror for rulers.' A king speaks in it; and he solemnly professes his resolve not, like many an Eastern ruler, to make his palace the home of caprice, and self-indulgence, and corruption, and favouritism, but to walk within his house in the integrity of his heart, to set no base example before his eyes, to cherish no crooked purpose, or evil design, to tolerate around him no slander or pride or injustice, but to make men of probity and integrity his companions and ministers, and finally morning by morning to hold his court of justice, that he may 'root out all wicked doers out of the city of the Lord.' And so this Psalm is naturally appointed as one of the Proper Psalms for the day of the Sovereign's accession.

I have been led to refer this morning to

LXXII] THE PSALMS

these ideals of kingly rule, on account of the great national event which is to take place next Thursday. More than a year has indeed elapsed since our gracious Sovereign assumed the throne : but it is the striking and impressive coronation ceremony which seals and ratifies his accession, and formally entrusts to him the high duties and the high responsibilities which in his august office he is called upon to perform. Circumstances have indeed changed greatly since the poets and prophets of Israel wrote. In those days absolute monarchies were the usual form of government in the East ; they were indeed the only practicable form of government, in times when the culture and education of the people were limited, when what we should call the political life of a nation had not yet begun to assert itself, and the influence of the people upon such subjects as legislation, the treatment of social problems, and national policy, was practically *nil*. But an absolute monarchy is no longer suited to the wide and varied needs and interests of modern civilization : hence the monarchies which have continued to the present day are mostly limited in power to a far greater extent than was the case in antiquity ; the power of the people, as represented in parliamentary assemblies and other ways, has greatly increased ; while in many nations democracies have supplanted monarchies altogether. But whether the government be a monarchy, or an oligarchy, or a democracy, all governments are constituted to maintain the welfare of the people governed by them ; and hence the great principles of righteousness and equity and justice, on which the prophets so eloquently insist, and of which the Psalmists sing, remain as the foundations of a prosperous state, and as the essential conditions of its people's welfare. ' Righteousness,' says a Hebrew proverb, ' exalteth a nation. But sin is a reproach to peoples.' And all history shows the truth of this generalisation, whatever be the form of government by which the nation is ruled.

It is true, of course, that, the power and rights of the Crown being in modern countries limited and the population and area of a country like our own, for instance, being so

THE PSALMS

much greater than those of ancient Israel, the Sovereign cannot interfere directly, or act personally, to the extent that he did there ; he cannot, for instance, like David and Solomon, himself administer justice, or himself introduce reforms, or determine, with merely the approval of a few counsellors, questions of peace and war : but he can do a great deal indirectly ; he can, in virtue of his high position and the respect which it commands, influence public opinion, and contribute materially to maintain high standards of responsibility and honour, on the part of his ministers ; he can mark with his approval men of efficiency and high character ; he can by suggestion and example encourage and promote social reforms. Power need not be less real, because it is wielded indirectly. Certainly the most crying evils of an Oriental monarchy, the abuse of power and position on the part of high officials, the extortion and oppression practised by them upon the poor and the defenceless, and the selling of justice to the highest bidder, are, happily, unknown in this country, and do not therefore need a sovereign to put them down. But there are still, it must sorrowfully be confessed, many social abuses rife among the less responsible classes of the community— among the wealthy, for instance, luxury and selfishness are more prevalent than they should be, and among the middle classes the love of gain leads often both to impositions upon those who are least able to bear them, and to the terrible abuse commonly described as 'sweating'; these can only be effectively rectified by moving public opinion; and in contributing towards this end, the indirect influence of the Sovereign may be of supreme value. The Sovereign is still the head of the State, though he acts largely not personally, but through the agency of ministers, judges, and other representatives, whose appointments are either made or sanctioned by himself. And so in the coronation ceremony, the sword, the symbol of judgement and of the power to maintain order, to put down misgovernment, and to punish evil-doers, is presented upon the altar with a prayer, the terms of which are suggested by words of St. Paul (Rom.

xiii. 4), and St. Peter (1 Pet. ii. 14), 'Hear our prayers, O Lord, we beseech Thee, and so direct and support Thy servant, our king, who is now to be girt with this sword, that he may not bear it in vain ; but may use it as the minister of God for the terror and punishment of evil-doers, and for the protection and encouragement of those that do well ; through Jesus Christ our Lord' ; and afterwards, when it has been girt about him, the Sovereign is addressed in these words : ' With this sword do justice, stop the growth of iniquity, protect the holy Church of God, help and defend widows and orphans, restore the things that are gone to decay, maintain the things that are restored, punish and reform what is amiss, and confirm what is in good order ; that doing these things you may be glorious in all virtue ; and so faithfully serve our Lord Jesus Christ in this life, that you may reign for ever with Him in the life which is to come,' and the Sceptre, the ' ensign of kingly power and justice ' is delivered to him with these words : ' Receive the Rod of equity and mercy : and God, from whom all holy desires, all good counsels, and all just works do proceed, direct and assist you in the administration and exercise of all those powers which He has given you. Be so merciful that you be not too remiss; so execute justice that you forget not mercy. Punish the wicked, protect and cherish the just, and lead your people in the way wherein they should go.'

These then are the high responsibilities which our Sovereign undertakes—to maintain effectually justice and good government, to temper wisely judgement with mercy, to have a care for true religion, to defend the unprotected, to punish evil-doers and in general to check iniquity, to correct anomalies and abuses, to guard and preserve whatever may contribute to the well-being of the people. Expanded and enlarged, these are just the same responsibilities which, in the two Psalms which I have quoted this morning, constitute the ideal of a king. Let us be thankful that we in this country are ruled by a Sovereign who, as we well know, will respect and maintain the noble traditions of high endeavour and high achievement which he has inherited from his ancestors, who will devote himself heart and soul to the task of realising, as far as in him lies, the great ideal which the Coronation Service sets before him, and who, with God's help, will pass on to his successors an empire, embracing far-stretching regions in every quarter of the globe, not less stable, and not less well-ordered and well-governed, than it was when he received it from his beloved and honoured father.

PSALM LXXIII

PSALM LXXIII

Nevertheless I am continually with thee :
  Thou hast holden my right hand ;
Thou shalt guide me with Thy counsel,
  and afterward receive me with glory.
Whom have I in heaven but Thee ?
  and there is none upon earth that I desire beside
    Thee.
My flesh and my heart faileth ;
  but God is the rock of my heart and my portion
    for ever. (Psalm lxxiii. 23-26.)

THE ideas of a future life entertained by the ancient Israelites were dim and uncertain. They did not indeed suppose that the soul, after death, ceased to exist, but their belief respecting the state into which it then passed was very different from that which is taught in the New Testament. In fact, we seem in most parts of the Old Testament to have on this subject no revelation, but simply allusions to the beliefs or opinions current among the people. The popular belief was that all passed alike into the unseen world; life did not cease after death: but it was shadowy, unreal, ghostlike. The righteous and the wicked shared all alike. The unseen realm, in which the souls of the deceased were assembled, bore the name of Sheol, a name which occurs often in the Revised Version of the Old Testament, and which corresponds to the Greek Hades. It is also sometimes represented by the word *Hell* which, however, must here be understood (as always in the Old Testament) not as denoting the place of torment, but in the wider and more general sense which, to avoid misunderstanding, might perhaps be better expressed by the term *Underworld*. All meet in Sheol, as when Jacob says, 'For I will go down to Sheol unto my son mourning,' or as when it is said of the company of Korah that the earth opened its mouth and they went down alive into Sheol. And so Job, when, in the 3rd chapter of his book, he curses the day of his birth and wishes that he had been carried at once from the womb to the grave, exclaims passionately

LXXIII] THE PSALMS

that then he would have slept and been at rest with kings and counsellors of the earth, with princes that had gold and filled their houses with silver, where 'the wicked cease from troubling, and the weary are at rest, where the prisoners are at ease together, and hear not the voice of the task-master.' In the 14th chapter of the Book of Isaiah the prophet draws a fine imaginative description of the Underworld, the kings who lived on earth in state being represented as still invested with the same dignity after death, seated on their thrones, and rising to greet ironically the stranger, the proud King of Babylon whom the prophet sees destined shortly to join them. And there is a similar striking representation in Ezekiel xxxii., where the prophet pictures the king of Egypt and all his multitude brought down to Sheol, and there joining the hosts of other kingdoms—Assyria, Elam, Tubal, Meshech, Edom, and the Zidonians, all at rest, each in their own special abode, in the vast recesses of the Underworld. In these exceptional cases the chief elements in the picture are no doubt due to the prophets investing the popular conception with imaginative traits. But there are many passages which attest the general opinion of the lot of man after death, in a dark and shadowy abyss, where the soul is cut off from God, and the voice of praise is hushed ; in the Book of Job,

> Are not my days few ? cease then :
>   And let me alone, that I may take comfort a little ;
> Before I go whence I shall not return,
> Even to the land of darkness, and the shadow of death ;
> A land of thick darkness, as darkness itself,
> A land of the shadow of death, without any order,
> And where the light is as darkness.

Elsewhere in the same book man's future after death is expressed yet more darkly :

> There is hope for a tree, if it be cut down, that it will sprout again,
> Though the root thereof wax old in the earth
> And the stock thereof die in the ground ;
> Yet through the scent of water it will bud,
> And bring forth boughs like a plant.
> But man dieth and wasteth away :
> Yea, man giveth up the ghost, and where is he ?
> The waters fail from the sea,

LXXIII]   THE PSALMS

  And the river decayeth and drieth up ;
  So man lieth down and riseth not ;
  Till the heavens be no more they shall not awake,
  Nor be roused out of their sleep.

And in verses that follow Job declares passionately his readiness to remain in Sheol, to which he knows he must ultimately come, as long as needful, if only he might thereby recover God's favour. But this is regarded by him as conditioned by a return to life, which he does not treat as a possibility : and so the momentary gleam of hope passes from him.

In the Psalms, the same representation is found more than once—in the 6th Psalm,

>   Return, O Lord, deliver my soul :
>   Save me, for Thy loving-kindness' sake :
>   For in death there is no remembrance of Thee,
>   In Sheol who shall give Thee thanks ?

And again,

  What profit is there in my blood, when I go down to
      the pit ?
  Shall the dust praise Thee ? shall it declare Thy
      truth ?

And in a still more decisive strain—

> Wilt Thou show wonders to the dead ?
> Shall the shades arise and praise Thee ?
> Shall Thy loving-kindness be declared in the grave ?
>   or Thy faithfulness in Destruction ?
> Shall Thy wonders be known in the dark ?
>   and Thy righteousness in the land of forgetfulness ?

And in the Song of Hezekiah in Isa. xxxviii.

> For the grave cannot praise Thee, death cannot celebrate Thee ;
>   they that go down into the pit cannot hope for Thy truth.
> The living, the living, he shall praise Thee, as I do this day,
>   the father, and the children shall make known Thy faithfulness.

God is praised by His worshippers upon earth : but in the grave their voices are silent : the thought of returning from the darkness of the Underworld, of seeing God again in a future life whether upon earth or in heaven, seemed an all but impossible one. Existence after death was, as it were, a dreamy shadow of the life in the flesh ; it brought no compensation for the ills of life, no punishment for its sins.

THE PSALMS

This idea of death, however, as I said, is not the positive searching of revelation, it is the popular idea from which revelation starts, and revelation rather consists in exhibiting to us how it was partially overcome, and how the way was thus in the Old Testament gradually prepared for the fuller enunciation of the truth of immortality brought to light by Christ Jesus. The popular idea of death was transcended along three lines in the Old Testament. It was transcended by the prophets, who in their visions of the glorified Zion of the future sometimes pictured its inhabitants, though living on earth, as living with earthly limitations and disabilities removed, and so represented the power of death as restricted or even abolished altogether. It was transcended secondly by the idea of a resurrection, which may be traced in different parts of the Old Testament, as gradually growing, and attaining greater definiteness, and, even, in the Book of Daniel, including the different lot of the just and unjust. It was transcended thirdly—and this chiefly in the Psalms—by the faith of individual saints, which struggled with the ordinary popular conception, and sought to overcome it by demanding, and realizing, as faith does, its demand, that the communion with God enjoyed in life should not be terminated by death. And that is the thought expressed in the passage which I have taken for my text.

The Psalm deals with a difficulty which sometimes pressed heavily upon the pious person under the Old Dispensation, who knew only of this world as the scene of God's dealings with men, and missed the clear evidence of God's justice which they desired to see in the reward of the righteous and the punishment of the wicked. The difficulty was this: Why should good men suffer, and bad men prosper? For the reason that I have stated, the prospect of the inequality here being compensated after death scarcely presented itself to him as possible. God was a righteous judge, meting out to men in this world the due recompense of their deeds. The course of the world, where those who had cast off the fear of God were rich and powerful, made him ready to question this truth and was a serious stumbling-block to his faith. The same perplexity is dealt with in the 37th Psalm, as well as in the 73rd. In the 37th Psalm the advice given is to wait, to *hold thee still* in the Lord ; and the advice is based on the assurance that in the end the seeming disorder will be set right even in this world. The righteous are preserved from evil, and inherit the earth, while the enemies of Jehovah are cast down ; and the Psalmist instances, from his own experience, examples of their overthrow. But this solution is only partial and incomplete : it leaves out of consideration instances which conflict with it ; it might be justified by the experience to which the Psalmist appeals, but could not be regarded as of universal application. There remain too many instances of the wicked prospering, and of the righteous meeting with misfortunes even to the end of life.

In the 73rd Psalm the solution is partly that of Psalm xxxvii., partly that of Psalm xlix. Visible retribution does indeed overtake the ungodly ; but the Psalmist does not place over against this, on the other side, an earthly portion of honour and happiness for the just. Their portion is in God, who is the stay and satisfaction of their hearts now and will take them to Himself hereafter.

> Surely God is good to Israel,
>   even to them that are of a pure heart.

Thus at the beginning does he state, by way of Introduction, the conclusion to which his meditations had led him; he is convinced of the goodness of God to Israel, at least—for he immediately qualifies and limits the word—to those that are of a pure heart, to whom, as he feels, 'all things work together for good.'

He recounts next the story of the questionings which had assailed him, the temptation to which he had nearly succumbed, how his feet had almost gone; his treadings had well-nigh slipt. He was envious when he saw the prosperity of the wicked, how they came into no trouble like other men, and were not plagued as other folk, how in consequence pride encompassed their neck, and violence clad them about as a garment, and how their hearts overflowed with proud aims and immoderate ambitions, how their eyes stood out with fatness—a suggestive picture of the sleek countenance, the self-satisfied look which betokens the too successful men of the world —and how the imaginations of their heart overflowed—its proud aims and immoderate ambitions exceeded all bounds.

> They scoff, and talk of evil;
>   they talk of oppression from on high.[1]
> They have set their mouth in the heavens,
>   and their tongue walketh through the earth.

They talk as if they were gods, and dictate to men as though the earth belonged to them. And then in their pride and self-delusion they exclaim 'How doth God know? And is there

---

[1] [Here Dr. Driver adopts a division of the two clauses of the verse different from that which is embodied in the Hebrew text, taking the word which means 'oppression' from the first clause into the second. This rearrangement is demanded by the rhythm. According to the division of the clauses in the Hebrew text as it stands, the verse must be rendered—

> They scoff, and in wickedness utter oppression;
>   they speak loftily.]

knowledge in the Most High?' It is a singularly graphic and powerful picture. In a few strokes, this old Hebrew poet has sketched a character—that of the self-satisfied, supercilious, self-important man of the world—which will live for ever. What, we wonder, was his model for these unlovely traits? Can we venture to hope that the character never reappears in these days? Or must we be satisfied to think that it is not so conspicuous as it once was, does not attract so much attention, does not sit in the high places of the land? The sight, however, was one which moved the Psalmist greatly; and the bitter thought rose to his lips that his own integrity of life had brought him no advantage.

> Surely in vain have I cleansed my heart,
>   and washed mine hands in innocency;
> For all the day have I been plagued,
>   and chastened every morning.

These misgivings, though he refrains from uttering them, continued to trouble him until he went one day into the sanctuary, and there realized more vividly than he had done before *the latter end* of such men—the sudden reverses, the terrible overthrow which not unfrequently overtakes them in the very bosom of their prosperity.

> Surely thou dost set them in slippery places :
> Thou castest them down and destroyest them ;
> Oh, how suddenly do they consume,
> perish, and come to a fearful end !

The thought which dispels the Psalmist's doubts, and restores his faith, is not the lot of the ungodly beyond the grave (of which he knows nothing), not even the tormenting trouble of an evil conscience, but their sudden and irremediable fall in this world. The thought in which he finds consolation is this, that, though the wicked often continue to prosper, yet, looking upon their career as a whole, the fearful reverses which they sometimes experience are a testimony to the justice of God, and an indication that their prosperity is not in accordance with His purpose. And then he blames himself for having brooded upon his doubts so long, with such little insight into God's dealings with man, and attributes his having done so to the embitterment, discontent, and envy which the sight of apparent injustice aroused in his breast—

> For my heart grew bitter,
>   and I was pricked in my reins:
> So brutish was I, and ignorant,
>   I was as a beast before Thee.

But over against the fate of the wicked, he sets, not—like the writer of Psalm xxxvii.—the earthly happiness reserved for the just, but the higher thought of the love and favour with which he is sensible that he is himself regarded by God, a love and favour which he is conscious nothing can interrupt, a guidance which will continue throughout life, a strength and support which will never desert him—

> And yet, as for me, I am always with thee:
>   Thou hast holden my right hand.
> Thou wilt guide me with Thy counsel,
>   and afterward wilt receive me in glory.
> Whom have I in heaven but Thee?
>   and there is none upon earth that I desire in comparison of Thee.
> My flesh and my heart faileth:
>   but God is the rock of my heart and my portion for ever.

He is always 'with God', i.e., always in

His thought, an object of His care ; God holds him by his right hand, God guides him and will bring him to a glorious future ; in His providence he is secure ; in His strength, though bodily power fails, he is conscious of an abiding support ; in God he rejoices as in his great and only possession. And so he concludes that ' to draw near to God is good ' —departure from God is death and destruction, in His presence and in nearness to Him are to be found joy and safety. The poet, as a recent commentator has finely said, has passed through ' one of those exalted moments, in which " heaven's morning breaks." Having God, earth has become a heaven. What more could heaven itself give him ? '

But we notice even here the reserve with which the Psalmist speaks about the future. He does not speak of it in the explicit, ecstatic terms which would have been used by one of the Apostles of our Lord. His words might even be understood not to include a reference to life hereafter at all. For instance, the expression *for ever* in the Old Testament often denotes no more than the whole term of earthly existence. But viewed as a whole, the expectation of the Psalmist certainly seems to reach beyond the present. The passage is one of the few occurring in the Psalms—the others being in the 16th, 17th and 49th Psalms—in which the ordinary belief of Old Testament saints is transcended, the limits by which their vision was ordinarily confined are broken through and faith with bold assurance rises to the thought of a communion with God superior to death and not severed by it. But the conviction of a future life is not appealed to by the Psalmist as an established dogma: it is expressed as an aspiration, a conviction, a demand which the Psalmist's faith cannot but make, and which he feels will be realized.

What, we may ask, is the origin of the difficulty which troubled the Psalmist? A little reflection will show that it arises out of the fact that it has pleased God that the course of the world should be carried on by general laws, with the operation of which He does not, as a rule, interfere. Hence the same lines of conduct lead regularly to similar consequences. The wicked man sometimes prospers, because he possesses qualities of cleverness or wealth or position which command success; though cases, as we all know, occur in which he overreaches himself, and one of those signal reverses befalls him which arrest the attention of the onlooker, and which so forcibly impressed the Psalmist. The righteous man again sometimes encounters misfortune, because he fails in those qualities which bring worldly prosperity, or because circumstances beyond his control affect him unfavourably. The Jew pictured God as regulating *directly* the course of the world: he did not clearly perceive that society, and the changes which take place in society, were regulated by Him in accordance with fixed laws, or, in other words, by means of those fixed and stated principles which we term natural; and hence he was surprised that God did not interfere in His capacity of judge of the earth and rectify the anomalies which He sometimes saw around Him. But to interfere in this way would be to destroy the entire system on which the world is constituted, and to neutralize one of the great educational forces of the world. For changes of fortune may test and purify character. It is of course only too true that cases which arouse our keenest sympathies have probably been known to most of us, that changes of fortune may involve those who are morally irreproachable in what we term great hardships. But we must remember, firstly, that sometimes those who suffer are responsible themselves for misfortunes which overtake them, and that by the exercise of the worldly virtues of prudence and foresight they might avert or lessen them; and, secondly, that the degree of suffering which a change of fortune occasions depends largely upon the temper in which it is met, and that if received in an attitude of resignation, or regarded as a mode in which God chastens—as a father—those whom He loves, it may be robbed of its sting, and may even bring a blessing with it.

The Psalmist, however, does not pursue the subject into these reflections, except indirectly. He does not say whether he himself has experienced misfortune or not. He only tells us of the perplexity which the overweening prosperity of the wicked occasioned to him, and of the observation which satisfied his doubts. For his own part, if adversity has been his lot, he does not complain ; if prosperity, he makes no boast of it. He finds his satisfaction elsewhere. He has been raised himself, and he raises us, into a region unperturbed by the changes and chances of this earthly life. We are lifted by his words above fears and doubts and perplexities ; we breathe with him the air of heaven. He does not indeed use the glowing language which St. Paul, writing in the light of a fuller revelation, would employ ; but, if he did not enjoy that fuller revelation, his faith and hope only stand out in clearer relief.

' He rises victorious over the world of sense and appearance in the inward certainty of the reality of his communion with God, and the conviction that this is the highest good and the truest happiness of which man is capable.'[1] The contrast, it should always be remembered, drawn in the Old Testament is not between

[1] Kirkpatrick, *ad loc.*, *Cambridge Bible*, p. 438.

life here and life hereafter (the hope of which, as I have said before, was in the Old Testament very dim), but between life on earth with God, and without God : life on earth with God and a sense of communion with Him was to the Old Testament saints a source of the purest happiness and delight ; life without God was to them of all things most miserable. That present sense of communion with Him was in most cases all for which they felt either a desire or a need. But now and again they looked beyond it ; and the conviction pressed itself upon them that the blessedness of fellowship with God could not be suddenly interrupted by death, but must be continued afterwards. The present is perhaps one of the most striking of the many devotional passages in which the unnamed poets of Israel express their sense of the consolation which they derive from the thought of God, and their vivid consciousness of His presence and help. That consciousness sustains them, whether in times of national calamity or danger—' though the earth be moved, and though the hills be carried into the midst of

the sea '—or of personal weakness and failure—
' though my flesh and my heart fail, yet God is the rock of my heart and my portion for ever.' It is their support in sorrow, as it is their delight in prosperity.

May we make the Psalmist's temper our own, and in times when difficulties perplex, or troubles vex, find our strength in the assurance that God is with us, that He is guiding us with His counsel here, and will receive us in glory hereafter.

INDEX

Aaron, 132, 194
Abraham, 87
Ahab, 78, 85
Akra, the, 124
Alexander Balas, 123
Aloes, 85
Annexed Prayer Book, 8, 10
Antiochus Epiphanes, 123
Atomistic style of Biblical interpretation, 47

Babylonian exile, 137; return from, 184
Barak, 121
Barnes, W. E., 30
Bäthgen, F., 29, 53, 68, 69, 111, 125, 126, 138, 149, 156, 174, 177, 178 f., 196
Bertholet, A., 64 ff.
Bickell, G., 176
Bishops' Bible, 7
Booths, feast of, 123
Briggs, C. A., 63, 111, 184
Bruce, A. B., 29
Bruston, C., 174
Burney, C. F., 42, 123, 207

Carleton, J. G., 30
Cassia, 85
Cheyne, T. K., 30, 37, 56, 64, 80, 118, 123, 138, 149, 160, 174, 176 f., 196, 199
Christ, fulfilling ideals of Psalms, 21 f., 23, 24 ff., 71 f., 131, 152, 185 f., 208 ff., 243
Church, R. W., 30
Communion with God, 189 ff., 294 ff.
Complaint, Psalms of, 155 f.
Consistency, 251
Coronation of King George V, 270 f.; ceremony of, 274 ff.
Coverdale, Miles, 3, 4, 5, 11, 34, 87
Cromwell, Thomas, 3, 4

Crown, modern functions of the, 272 ff.
Cyrus, 145

Daniel, book of, 287
David, 67, 68, 69, 73, 80, 94, 98, 122, 129, 135, 179 f., 269 f., 273; Psalms ascribed to, 13, 42, 129 ff., 209, 231; promise given to, 56; dynasty of, 57, 111
Davies, T. Witton, 123
Davison, W. T., 26, 29
Death, popular idea of, transcended in Old Testament, 287
Delitzsch, Franz, 194
Delitzsch, Friedrich, 54, 65
Deutero-Isaiah, 103, 146, 171, 180, 182 f.
Deuteronomy, 141, 142, 169
Duhm, B., 53, 98, 190

Edghill, E. A., 21, 22, 83, 123, 131 f., 209
Elijah, 124, 226
Ely, Dean of, 152; *see also* Kirkpatrick, A.F.
Ezekiel, 110

'Faithfulness,' 145
'Flesh,' 199
Footstool, figure of, 116
Future life; *see under* Life

Gentiles, conversion of, 23, 172, 180, 182, 186
Gibson, F., 7, 9
'Glory,' 199
'Goodness,' meaning of term, 247 f.
Government, of the world, the Divine, 221 f., 297; forms of human, 271 f.

INDEX

Gray, G. B., 38, 53
Great Bible, 3, 4, 5, 7, 9, 10, 11, 87
Greek period, 70
Gressmann, H., 82
Gunkel, H., 57

Halévy, J., 160
Headlam, A. C., 72
Hezekiah, Song of, 286
Hitzig, F., 63, 190
Holiness, of God, 158
Houbigant, C. F., 190
Human element in Bible, 224 ff.
Hupfeld, H., 138, 147, 176, 178

'I,' collective, in Psalms, 18 f., 150, 155 ff., 180 f.
Ideal future, 170 f.; ideal character, 248 ff.; ideal of fellowship, 209
'Imprecatory' Psalms, 26 ff., 213 ff.
Inspiration, theory of Biblical, 224 f.

Jacob, 108
James, M. R., 71, 127 f.
Jastrow, M., 65
Jehoram of Judah, 77
Jehoshaphat, 122
Jeremiah, 27, 28, 110, 129, 217 ff.
Joarib, 125
Job, book of, 284 f.
Jonathan, son of Saul, 121; brother of Judas Maccabaeus, 123, 125 f.
Joshua, 116
Josiah, 109, 265
Judas Maccabaeus, 123
'Judgement,' 182 f.

Kautzsch, E., 38, 180
Kennedy, A. R. S., 57, 90 f.
Kimchi, David, 170
King, in Psalms, 20 f., 51 ff., 77 ff., 97 ff., 115 ff., 265 ff.; representing nation, 58; Messianic, 68 ff., 82, 93, 102, 110 f., 126 ff., 130, 269 ff.
Kirkpatrick, A. F., 5, 26, 29, 63, 90, 107, 111, 130, 174, 179, 190, 200, 207, 299
Kittel, R., 39 f.

Lagarde, P. de, 53, 64, 107
Lagrange, M. J., 66
Life, path of, 202 f.; future, in Old Testament, 205 ff., 222, 281 ff.
'Liver,' as seat of mental impulses, 199 f.
Lupton, J. H., 12

Maccabees, the, 123 ff.
McGarvey, W., 7
Magog, 68
Man, conception of, 231 ff.
Marduk, 66
Margins, importance of, in R.V., 36 f.
Matthew, Thomas, 3
Matthew's Bible, 4, 5
Melchizedek, 120, 129, 131
Mendelssohn, 166
Messiah; see under King, Messianic.
Messianic element in Psalms, 20 ff., 150 f., 208; see also under Psalms.
Milton, 118
Mozley, F. W., 143
Münster, Sebastian, 4, 5, 6, 15, 45

'Name,' force of, in Hebrew, 167, 234
Nation of Israel individualized, 18 f., 180 f., 185; see also 'I,' collective.
Nature, Psalms of, 232
New Testament quotations; see under Psalms.
Nowack, W., 174, 178 f.

Oesterley, W. O. E., 30
Ottley, R. L., 30

Parallel Psalter, 8, 11, 12, 29, 35 f., 45, 66, 87, 88, 146, 161, 192
Paul, Saint, 299
Perowne, J. J. S., 23, 25, 26, 29, 236
Peter, Saint, 209
Pharisees, 127, 130
Prayer Books, First and Second of Edward VI, 6
Prayer Book Version of Psalms, sources of, 3 ff.; relation of

INDEX

to Great Bible Psalter, 7 ff.;
style and character of, 11 ff.;
need for revision of, 34 f.
Progressive revelation in Old
Testament, 28, 213 ff., 225 f.
Prophetic perfect, 173
Prothero, R. E., 30
Psalms, dates and authors of, 12
ff.; personal situation implied
in, 14 f., 43 ff.; religious value
of, 16 f.; canons of interpretation of, 17 f.; speaker in,
18 f.; Messianic, 20 f., 70 ff.,
93; ideal features of, 22 f.;
application distinct from interpretation, 24 f.; 'imprecatory,'
26 ff., 213 ff.; use made of
in New Testament, 48, 71 ff.,
82, 129 f., 132, 142 f., 151 f.,
208, 243
Psychology of Hebrews, 140 f.,
142, 197
Ptolemies, the, 111

Rabbinical Bible, 39
Rahab, 138
Rehoboam, 92
'Reins,' 197
Representative character of certain Psalms, 19, 22, 149, 155 ff.
Resurrection, hope of, 206; *see
also under* Life, future.
'Righteousness,' 145, 175
Ryle, H. E., 71, 127 f.

Sacrifice, conception of, in Psalms,
140
'Salvation,' Hebrew words for,
145

Sanday, W., 29
Sarah, 87
Saul, 213
Sealed Books, 8, 10, 87
Seba, 104, 267
Septuagint, the, 40, 186; mistranslations of, 208
Servant of Jehovah, 19, 182 f., 185
Sheba, 104, 267
Sheol, 201, 203, 205 f., 282 ff.
Sievers, E., 65
Simon, brother of Judas Maccabaeus, 123 ff.
Skinner, J., 175, 183, 199
Smith, W. Robertson, 195, 196
'Sojourn,' meaning of, 249
Solomon, 57, 67, 69, 77, 80, 86,
101 f., 105, 110, 116, 129, 266,
270, 273; Psalms of, 70, 127 f.
Suffering, problem of, 155 ff.

Tarshish, 103, 105, 267
Tiglath Pileser I, 165
Tindale, William, 3
Truth, 252
Tyre, daughter of, 88 f.

Usury, condemned by ancient
writers, 256 ff.
Uzziah, 122

Vulgate, the, 38, 87

Wâdy, 121
Westcott, B. F., 12, 29, 73, 87, 143
Whewell, W., 236
Whitehouse, O. C., 183
Wright, W. A., 12
Wünsche, A., 62

www.ingramcontent.com/pod-product-compliance
Lightning Source LLC
Chambersburg PA
CBHW050336230426
43663CB00010B/1873